JAZZ IN THE SIXTIES

D0067298

JAZZ

IN
THE
SIXTIES

The Expansion of Musical Resources and Techniques

Michael J. Budds

AN EXPANDED EDITION

UNIVERSITY OF IOWA PRESS
IOWA CITY

ML
3506
.B8
1990

University of Iowa Press, Iowa City 52242
Copyright © 1990 by the University of Iowa
All rights reserved
Printed in the United States of America
First edition, 1990

No part of this book may be reproduced or
utilized in any form or by any means,
electronic or mechanical, including
photocopying and recording, without
permission in writing from the publisher.

Printed on acid-free paper

*Library of Congress
Cataloging-in-Publication Data*

Budds, Michael J., 1947–
    Jazz in the sixties: the expansion of musical
    resources and techniques/by Michael J.
    Budds. — An expanded ed.
        p.   cm.
    Includes bibliographical references.
    ISBN 0-87745-281-4 paper (alk. paper)
    1. Jazz music.   2. Jazz music — Analysis,
    appreciation.   I. Title.
    ML3506.B8   1990   89-20669
    781.65'09'046 — dc20   CIP   MN

Some material in this book © 1961 by Prestige
Records and © 1969 by Fantasy Records.

cbd8885
cbd8885

Dedicated to my mother,

my brother,

and my sister

and to the memory of my father

Contents

List of Musical Examples

Preface

Because the scholarly study of jazz is a relatively recent development, the musicological literature on the topic is by no means considerable. What does exist is focused primarily on the music and musicians of the earliest periods in the history of jazz. Gunther Schuller's *Early Jazz* (New York: Oxford University Press, 1968) until recently was the only grand scale, fully documented study of jazz to date. Frank Tirro's *Jazz: A History* (New York: Norton, 1977) was not available when this was written. The only scholarly journals devoted to this music are *Jazzforschung* (founded 1969) and the *Journal of Jazz Studies* (founded 1974). There is, however, an enormous body of popular and trade literature that chronicles the entire lifespan of jazz. In many instances the enthusiasm of reporters for their subject matter is a poor excuse for an understanding of the music they attempt to describe, but these often highly-opinionated writings were not intended to be judged by scholarly criteria and are valuable in the absence of critical studies.

In my research on the jazz produced during the sixties, this genre of journalistic criticism has provided important background material that would have been otherwise unavailable. The American jazz magazine *down beat* and its English counterpart *Jazz Journal* have been indispensable aids. The information located on record jackets, while often sensational, has been another important resource. Of the major studies of the period, *Free Jazz* by Ekkehard Jost (Graz: Universal, 1974) is especially authoritative on the music of the black avant-garde. Another recent publication, *The Jazz Book* by Joachim-Ernst Berendt (New York: Lawrence Hill, 1975) is a remarkable collection of information on all aspects of jazz, but is somewhat invalidated by its lack of documentation and the questionable perceptions of its author. Gerard Béhague's study of the *bossa nova* (*Ethnomusicology* 17, 1973) was essential for clarifying the general misinformation on that topic propagated by jazz journalists. The writings of Gunther Schuller and Martin T. Williams are also always perceptive and well informed. Many of the ideas set forth in the following discussion, however, are the results of my own listening and analysis.

The matter of dating recordings has been particularly problematical. Dates are usually not provided on recordings. Greater confusion is caused by the fact that the dates presented in the literature may be either the date of the recording session or the date of the issuing of a recording. Whenever possible, I have provided the date of the recording session. In other cases, the date given is an approximation based on the *Schwann Catalog,* the *National Union Catalog: Music and Phonorecords,* and other reliable sources. Therefore, the inclusion of the dates was not intended as an end in itself, but rather as a relative guide to the appearance of the recordings. I have also consistently italicized the titles of recordings and placed the titles of individual pieces in quotation marks.

Because of its focus on the innovative elements of jazz during the sixties, this study is not intended to serve as a general history of jazz for that period. The stylistic manifestations of the new attitudes toward jazz-making which prevailed during those years, however, do qualify this music more than any other single feature. Indeed not all avenues of experimentation were equally successful or influential, but, in addition to documenting these efforts, I have sought to evaluate significance and influence. The frequent references to recordings are inserted to illustrate my observations and to guide the reader to the music itself.

I would like to thank Professors Edward L. Kottick and Albert T. Luper of the University of Iowa for their guidance and assistance. I would also like to acknowledge my debt to Kit Craig, whose enthusiasm for jazz first sparked my interest in this music; to Dr. Sanford M. Helm, professor emeritus at California State University — Long Beach, who shared his knowledge of jazz and music in general with me and encouraged me to investigate this topic; and to my family, who made my graduate education possible.

Preface to the Expanded Edition

The invitation from Paul Zimmer, director of the University of Iowa Press, to make additions to this book was especially appealing because I had realized for a long time that the original edition had not addressed an important aspect of the topic — the purposes assigned to jazz by its creators during the cultural cauldron of the sixties. In addition, it presented the opportunity to organize my thoughts on the significance of the notable developments in jazz during the sixties from the vantage point of more than ten years later. Although I had thought about this music regularly in the intervening years and had continued to listen to it, I had not done so systematically. To be able to return to it for this purpose was especially gratifying.

This work was not originally conceived as a comprehensive history of jazz during the sixties. Nor have the additions been prepared in this light. The innovations and the departures from tradition during that period represent, at least in my mind, significant features of the music worth surveying and codifying.

I happily declare my special thanks to N. Jane Lohr, Dr. Marian Ohman, Dr. James M. Burk, Dr. J. Quentin Kuyper, and R. Kit Craig for their good-natured criticisms and helpful suggestions.

Survey of Jazz Styles Before 1960

From its beginnings around the turn of the century until the late fifties, the musical language of jazz was governed by a system of fundamental agreements that regulated a number of basic compositional matters and allowed performers to concentrate on improvisation. Jazz began as a distinctive manner of performing pre-existing music and, to a large degree, remained so throughout this period. Thus, its general framework was almost completely defined by the nature of the borrowed material, which included spirituals, hymns, marches, blues, dance tunes, and popular songs.

These models were part of a melody-oriented music that reflected a distillation of nineteenth-century European achievements and middle-class American tastes. A straightforward melody served as a possible basis for thematic improvisation, and the harmony it implied suggested the architectural chordal progressions of each repeated strophe. The harmonic content was one firmly grounded on European functional harmony, often in its most elementary form. The metric organization of the melody provided the pattern of recurrent stress that would also govern the improvisation. The effectiveness of the characteristic rhythmic liberties found in jazz renditions, in fact, depended upon the presence of this stress pattern. The choice of instruments for jazz performance was also determined by European practice.

Gunther Schuller's argument that jazz developed out of a simplification of African musical practice, "that every musical element — rhythm, harmony, melody, timbre, and the basic forms of jazz — is essentially African in background and derivation" and "that the Negro allowed European elements to become integrated into his Africa heritage,"[1] does not deny, however, the presence and importance of a musical substructure that is

European. In addition, then, to what must be considered the European contributions to the jazz performance framework, there were several equally important concepts retained or modified from African musical practice.

The first African retention was the matter of role assignment or the distribution of labor within the musical ensemble. In African music, such assignments are mainly concerned with rhythmic functions. In jazz, a harmonic consideration is also present. Each instrument was assigned to either a rhythm group or a melody group. The rhythm group, known in jazz as the "rhythm section," was responsible for presenting the essence of the model by providing its meter, by setting forth its harmonic architecture, and by keeping time. Members of the rhythm group usually included the drums, a bass instrument (tuba or string bass), and a "chording" instrument (banjo, guitar, or piano). The melody group, comprised of melody instruments, was responsible for delivering melodies and counter-melodies within the harmonic context and for providing layers of rhythmic interest above the fixed foundation.

Although the metric organization of jazz was conditioned by the restrictions of the European models, rhythmic conception and rhythmic detail were not. The so-called "hot rhythm" that makes jazz unlike any other form of Western music is the result of the presence of the property of "swing"[2] and of a process by which "European" weak beats are emphasized at the expense of strong beats. Schuller's characterization of the latter as a "'democratization' of rhythmic values"[3] is misleading because it implies even stress.

"Swing" is, perhaps, the most problematical term in the jazz lexicon. In spite of the efforts of numerous writers, a satisfactory definition of what swing is does not exist. The difficulty in identifying this unique property of jazz is unquestionably related to the fact that its perception is determined by the presence of a complex musical context, a combination of musical stimuli. Along such lines Schuller has described swing by isolating two characteristics he considers foreign to European fine-art music:

> (1) a specific type of accentuation and inflection with which notes are played or sung, and (2) the continuity — the forward-propelling directionality — with which individual notes are linked together.[4]

His extended discussion of this topic and his attempt to document its African origin are valuable contributions to the literature.

Swing then is the product of a non-European attitude toward music-making. In a sense it is the summary effect of various jazz performance practices involving the following: the placement of pitches within the metric framework, the color and inflection of the pitch itself, the relationship of the pitch to its neighbors, the articulation of the pitch, and possibly other musical phenomena equally difficult to ascertain and measure. The frequent reliance upon syncopation and the development of a variety of articulations were manifestations of the jazz musician's concern for nurturing this aspect of his music. The resulting sense of timing and foreground disregard for European stress patterns were essential features of the jazz musician's approach to the European models.

Another Africanism in jazz is the presence of a heterogeneous sound ideal. Instrumentation is manipulated to produce contrast in timbre and register. The stratification by levels of rhythmic activity, especially in early jazz, was another means of assuring the integrity of individual lines. The great variety of timbral effects, phrasing idiosyncrasies, and non-European methods of tone production also served this purpose.

From time to time, the influence of European ideals of homogeneous sound and precision has diminished this aspect of jazz performance practice. But even in the white bands of the Swing Era, in which the individualism of tone and expression was less prominent, the soli sections were still exploited for their intrinsic value and for their idiomatic differences. Closely allied to the notion of the heterogeneous sound ideal is the primacy of the improviser in jazz. The development of an individual "voice" has always been a major concern of jazz musicians. Unquestionably the masters were successful.

The pervasive influence of the blues represents another constant in the history of jazz performance. The blues is an indigenous American folk music created by blacks in the nineteenth century and crystallized into a specific chord and measure pattern by at least the early twentieth century. The singing style associated with the blues, its tradition of improvisation, and its harmonic formula have all been assimilated into the jazz style. Most important, however, was the incorporation of the blues tonality, the result of the liberal use of "blue" notes produced by flatting either the third, fifth, or seventh degree of a major scale. The blues must be seen as a significant precursor to the jazz style as well as an ever-present resource throughout its existence.

Finally, it is generally thought that black musicians imposed African formal elements onto the European substructure of jazz pieces (and other musical genres of Afro-American origin). The call-and-response pattern (antiphonal performance), the repeated refrain (the riff),[5] and the chorus format (series of variations) became standard methods for dealing with the thematic material in jazz performance. Each was important in creating the open conditions necessary for improvisation on the somewhat closed forms generated by functional harmony.

JAZZ STYLES BEFORE 1960

The following brief survey of jazz styles before 1960 is provided for the sake of background and perspective. An appreciation of the innovations of the sixties — a continuation of the evolutionary process, and the disintegration of the structural background — is dependent upon an understanding of the historical mainstream of jazz-making.

New Orleans Dixieland

The classic New Orleans dixieland band (ca. 1910 to ca. 1925) was the prototype of jazz ensembles. Its rhythm group consisted of the drums, banjo or guitar, tuba, and later piano. This rhythm section provided straightforward 4/4 meter, each instrument usually contributing on each of the four beats of the measure. The pace was constant. The melody group consisted of a trio of cornet, clarinet, and trombone. The cornet typically played the leading melody between a clarinet obbligato of smaller note values and a trombone counter-melody of longer note values cast in syncopated patterns.

The performance style was that of a disciplined group improvisation operating above a triadic substructure. The placement of the three relatively simple melodic lines above a non-melodic bass line created a three-part polyphonic texture, which remained in effect except in solo passages. Solo improvisation was generally ruled by the melodic paraphrasing of the original composition. Each chorus was developed out of embellishments of the theme in theme-and-variations format. The final chorus served as an emphatic climax, both in elaboration and intensity. Instrumental articulation and phrasing were in keeping with the vertical squareness of the accompaniment. With the exception of standard ragtime syncopations, accents were on the beat.

The sole opportunity for disregarding the given melody came in the "break," a short cadenza-like solo in strict time interpolated between ensemble passages. During the break, all members of the ensemble except the soloist stopped playing. He then delivered a melodic fragment with an anacrusis-like function over the implied meter and often an implied dominant tonality. The break, which was usually a two-measure unit, did not represent a departure from the organization of the pre-existing composition, but served as a connecting link between the conclusion of one chorus and the beginning of the next. Schuller contends that the solo break was an important evolutionary step in the development of the kind of harmonically-derived extended solo that would dominate later jazz styles.[6]

In spite of the rather well-defined conventions of the New Orleans dixieland style, a great variety of musical expression was achieved by its practitioners. Important figures of the period included King Oliver, Louis Armstrong, Jelly Roll Morton, Freddie Keppard, Bunk Johnson, and Sydney Bechet. The Original Dixieland Jazz Band and the New Orleans Rhythm Kings were ensembles that became especially well known.

Finally, it should be noted that the relationship of the early jazz band to the non-jazz marching band was very strong. In fact, these early jazz groups did play "on the march" — the colorful funeral parades are but one example.

Chicago Dixieland

A modification of the New Orleans style was found in the so-called Chicago style (ca. 1920 to ca. 1928). The most conspicuous changes were related to the rhythmic organization of the music and the development of the solo improvisation. Because of the social function of jazz as music for dancing, the 4/4 meter of the earlier style was replaced by an alla breve feeling known as the "two beat." Individual solo improvisations were given greater emphasis as the level of performer virtuosity increased and as, after the mid-twenties, the theme-improvisation concept was replaced by harmonic variation, the extemporizing upon chords rather than upon the melody. The style also exhibited faster tempos, smoother melodic contours, and frequently a greater number of complete triads. In general, however, the constant polyphonic density, the respect for prescribed instrumental duties and ranges, and the relative simplicity of melodic lines and the chords themselves remained unchanged.

This period in jazz history is noteworthy for the mature performances of trumpet player Louis Armstrong (1900–1971), one of the great soloists and innovators in the history of jazz. Armstrong excelled in delivering improvisations of great originality with an incomparable sense of swing and tone color. His most individual contribution was the imaginative use of an assortment of vibratos and shakes, devices employed to color single pitches. His solos became the example for content and technique and were widely imitated by his contemporaries, trumpet players as well as other instrumentalists.

Many other representatives of the previous New Orleans style remained active and participated in this transition from small-group jazz to large-ensemble jazz. A large number of white musicians reached prominence in the jazz world at this time. Trumpet player Bix Beiderbecke was, perhaps, the most illustrious of these.

Swing

Because jazz is primarily an improviser's art, the role of the arranger has never been as prominent as that of the player. With the small ensembles of early jazz, a piece of music was organized according to the conventions of the day. Specific details, or perhaps exceptions to the norms, were the products of preperformance verbal agreements. Such compositions were known as "head" arrangements. The delicate balance of dixieland collective improvisation, nevertheless, could not endure the weight of more complicated harmony and more technically proficient soloists. The weakening of earlier stylistic prescriptions and the addition of more instrumentalists to the jazz ensemble demanded the presence of the arranger/composer and the use of written arrangements. The saxophone had become a popular jazz instrument in the twenties, and a second trumpet had been an early addition to the dixieland nucleus. With the rise of instrumental "sections" — saxophone, trumpet, and trombone — the groundwork was laid for the supremacy of the big band in the thirties.

Once the jazz ensemble had lost the advantages of an intimate chamber ensemble, the arranger became the central figure in imposing order and providing guidance. The formerly continuous improvisation was now designated by the arranger to specific instrumentalists for specific choruses within the composition. The new possibilities for thematic statement and accompanimental passages — for controlling blocks of sound foreign to the earlier styles — posed problems that could only be solved by a semicompositional process. Arrangers, moreover, adopted an improvisatory style in written-out harmonizations for soli choruses. These developments in turn increased the demands for musical literacy among performers and charged them with overcoming the technical problems of uniform playing within sections. The opportunity for experimentation with orchestration, harmony, and musical structure also was expanded. The horizontal polyphonic aspect of the previous styles became less important as vertically conceived ensemble writing emerged.

In contrast then to the individualism and the self-realization of talented folk musicians which had characterized the dixieland styles, the subsequent period of large ensemble jazz exhibited the prominence of European aesthetic criteria. "Clean" rhythmic precision, "correct" intonation, symphonic tone quality, and a higher level of instrumental virtuosity became conspicuous artistic goals. This development was accompanied by, and surely closely related to, the participation in jazz-making of a sizable group of musicians, both black and white, who had received some training in music performance and music theory at American academic institutions and possessed some awareness of European fine-art music.

These circumstances resulted in considerable diversity within the greater stylistic unity. Individual bands quite naturally sought to establish their own identities, based on the idiosyncrasies of the bandleader, soloists, or arrangers. Racial differences can also be noted. The music of black big bands, such as those led by Fletcher Henderson with arranger Don Redman, Jimmy Lunceford, and Count Basie, often tended to maintain a closer relationship with the blues, emphasized solo improvisations of greater length, exhibited a greater variety of nuances and inflections in tone quality, and often relied upon the riff as the organizational device for ensemble passages. The music of white big bands, such as those led by Benny Goodman, Artie Shaw, and the Dorsey brothers, tempered by commercial success, revealed greater polish in their performances, exhibited a closer relationship to popular songs, and subordinated the jazz soloist to the arrangement to a much greater degree. The music of pianist and composer Duke Ellington (1899–1974) and his long-standing ensemble represents a special case. Ellington was successful in forging a personal style of great musical integrity and in delivering a series of original jazz masterpieces. A distinguishing factor in Ellington's music was his concern for the individual talents of his bandsmen and his incorporation of these strengths into his compositions.

In the big-band style, the rhythm section (drums, piano, string bass, and sometimes guitar) retained its function: defining meter, pulse, and harmonic foundation. The harmonic structure provided by the rhythm section was often re-enforced by the presence of written-out accompanimental passages for other instrumental sections, for example, the saxophone section or the trombone section. Rhythmic treatment was conditioned by the frequent use of 4/4 meter, emphasized by the presence of a quarter-note bass line performed in anticipation of each beat.

Bop

Dissatisfaction with the general precepts of the big-band style resulted in the birth of new jazz style in the early forties, a musical reaction that was not without social implications. Nurtured by a group of young black rebels, which included alto saxophonist Charlie Parker, trumpet player Dizzy Gillespie, pianist Thelonius Monk, and drummer Kenny Clarke, this music, known as "bop" or "bebop," was antithetical to the previous style. First of all, bop was not intended as a background for social dancing and was therefore released from the musical requirements of that function. It was small-group music, performed by a five- or six-member combo, in which the priorities of individual expression and the prerogatives of the improviser were reasserted. Subservience to the arranger and the need for his skills were nullified by a return to the theme-and-variations format and a reliance upon the blues and standard thirty-two-measure song forms. Performance tended to be virtuosic: very fast, well articulated, and asymmetrical.

Considerable use of chordal extensions and chord substitutions intensified the harmonic fabric. Corollary to these practices was the popularization of a "silent theme tradition,"[7] in which the harmonic structure of a popular song served as the basis of a jazz improvisation without its original melody ever being reproduced. A new melody in the contemporary improvisatory style replaced the original tune in the opening and closing choruses that framed solo improvisation. Thus, the original melody, although never heard, remained implied throughout the performance by the presence of its harmonic identity.

Because of the prevalence of faster tempos in the bop style, there was a tendency to equalize the unevenness of the Swing Era treatment of consecutive eighth notes. Off-beat accentuation, however, did not disappear. The sixteenth note became the rhythmic basis of improvisation.

One of the most far-reaching features of bop was the remodeling of the rhythm section, whose activities had remained substantially unchanged since the beginning of jazz. The string bass and the hi-hat cymbal were given time-keeping responsibilities, leaving the remainder of the drummer's trap set for accents and fills. The linear solo concept of the melody instruments was introduced into the right hand of the piano part. The chord changes no longer were delivered by the left hand of the piano part in a predictable manner, but more in the form of harmonic punctuation and accentuation. The bass line, of course, was provided by the string bass. Thus, in spite of the reduction of forces, the bop combo was capable of producing several layers of rhythmic-melodic interest and of filling the musical space. And, in spite of changes in ensemble organization, the rhythm group and melody group principle remained intact.

Big-band jazz was not, however, replaced by bop. It continued on its own course of development. Duke Ellington, considered to be one of the greatest jazz composers, produced a number of masterpieces in the now old-fashioned style after the "bop revolution."

Under the label of "Progressive Jazz," Stan Kenton and his imitators offered a type of big-band jazz most notable for its expansion of musical resources. Massive walls of sound were achieved by means of thick, redundant scoring and by expanding instrumental ranges. His ensemble now included six saxophones, five trumpets, four trombones, and a rhythm section. The "swing" element was minimized by a fascination with Afro-Cuban rhythms and percussion instruments. Solo improvisation was given a relatively minor role in many Kenton arrangements. The emphasis on orchestration, composition, volume, and sonority represents the fulfillment of certain aspects of the big-band style.

Cool

The bop style served as the point of departure for the two sub-styles that came into fashion in the fifties: cool and hard bop. The two sub-styles represent a polarity of emphasis within the same small-group context. The cool style, which appeared first, was characterized by a relaxation of intensity, a toning down of bop's drive and edge. This softening process was reflected in the acceptance of a subdued, controlled tone quality, breathy, often muted, and with little vibrato. Impressionistic-like harmonies became the favored vehicle for the accommodation of coloristic effects and pastel moods. Slower tempos permitted soloists to create long-lined, lyrical melodies. The rhythm section was encouraged to make coloristic contributions, such as the use of brushes on the snare drum and the use of the bow on the string bass. The popularity of triple meter (the jazz waltz) led to an interest in other meters, such as 5/4 and 9/8. The casting of jazz in structural designs borrowed from European art music, such as the rondo and the fugue, also appeared.

The effect of much cool jazz was one of calculation. This, combined with increased chromatic content, resulted in charges of intellectualism against the white musicians who were largely the exponents of the style. In addition, the favoring of sophisticated popular songs as models forced the blues, whose urgency and earthiness were inappropriate to the refined goals of cool, to a background position.

Hard Bop

Hard bop, also known as soul jazz, gospel jazz, and funky jazz, appeared around 1954, on the heels of the institutionalization of the cool style. Its proponents were mainly concerned with reaffirming the features of bop cast aside or minimized by the promoters of the cool style, features that can be summarized as the musical "blackness" of jazz. As practiced by black jazz artists, hard bop represented a return to basics, a return to the emotional content of earlier jazz, and a disregard for the "European" mannerisms of the rival style. It was strongly influenced by the "gospel" music of black Protestants and its rhythm-and-blues counterpart in entertainment music. The "gospel" sound was achieved by the frequent use of open fourths and fifths, the presence of the IV–I cadence and repetitive melodic units (recalling the riff), and the infrequent use of chromatic effects. The rich vocabulary of melodic nuances and inflections — the tradition of black vocal practice — was prominent. Off-beat accentuation was the characteristic rhythmic style trait.

Hard bop was not, however, immune to the purely musical advancements of the preceding style or to enlarging its expression on its own terms. The popular song was not discarded. It was, in fact, the combination of the popular song and the renewal of black expressive methods that typified the mainstream of jazz before the upheavals of the late fifties and early sixties. Jazz artists exhibited a mastery of improvising upon difficult harmonic progressions and of building cohesive solos by motivic development. Their ability to create metric ambiguity by manipulating foreground rhythmic details was unknown to any earlier period in the history of jazz.

The State of Jazz at the End of the Fifties

The stylistic changes that occurred in jazz before 1960 are manifestations of two closely related musical phenomena: the extension of the technical resources of soloists and an increase in the complexity of compositions accepted or modified for jazz treatment. Improvisational skills of jazz musicians have undergone an organic growth as each new generation of improvisers has based its own practice upon the experiments and accomplishments of established figures. According to Schuller, "it is virtually axiomatic that each succeeding jazz style has been nurtured on the conceptions of the immediately preceding generation of players. . . ."[8] The observations that standards of instrumental technique and improvisational skills have changed, have influenced subsequent jazz style, and have exhibited a progressive display of virtuosity should not, however, imply a value judgment.

Throughout this period a respect for the pre-existing thematic material or special compositions created as substitutes for this music was maintained. The triadic basis of the borrowed material continued to define the harmonic practice in jazz. The complexity of the chord vocabulary and the frequency of their appearance, the harmonic rhythm, did increase. By the end of the fifties, the harmonic language of jazz had been substantially enriched. Likewise, the metric organization of the models continued to define the metric organization of jazz pieces. Within the context of duple meter, the subdivision of the basic rhythmic pulse of improvisation changed from the eighth note of dixieland and swing to the sixteenth note of bop to the uneven groupettes of the late fifties. Experimentation with triple meter in the fifties opened the possibilities for the production of jazz in once-unconsidered metric patterns. At the same time the practice of disguising the metric framework of jazz renditions became progressively abstract.

In the jazz that would follow in the sixties, two courses of development can be identified. The first is a continuation of the kind of evolutionary process described in the preceding survey of jazz styles: musical exploration within the limitations of traditional performance methods. This would include the retention of pre-existing models as bases for improvisation, the maintenance of functional harmony, acceptance of the rhythm group and melody group division of labor, and a respect for a continuous pulse. This music would be distinctive, nevertheless, because of its own additions to and modifications of the inherited musical conventions.

The second course is concerned with the disintegration of

the structural background itself, in many cases an intentional assault on the rigidity of the historical framework. The new-found freedom, sought by "radicals" who considered the established practice used-up or worn-out, carried new responsibilities. The abandonment of once-assumed procedures demanded the re-evaluation of all aspects of jazz performance and their replacements by new systems of order. Emancipation from traditional practice first infiltrated the area of harmony, the area in which the restrictions appeared to be most severe. Melody, rhythm, meter, and structural design were subjected to similar scrutiny. Different forms of free group improvisation became the standard alternative.

The presence of these two contradictory attitudes toward music-making within the jazz community compounded by an awakening of interest in "world music," a new attempt to synthesize jazz and the music of the European fine-art tradition into a "Third Stream"[9] of music, the revitalization of the big band, and the continued incorporation of popular music into the jazz tradition created a stylistic diversity unprecedented in the history of jazz.

---

1   Gunther Schuller, *Early Jazz* (New York: Oxford University Press, 1968), p. 62.
2   This term is used here in its general sense, not in reference to its more specific use as a label for the big-band style of the thirties.
3   Schuller, *Early Jazz*, p. 6.
4   Schuller, *Early Jazz*, p. 7.
5   The riff is a repeated melodic motive borrowed from the blues tradition. Its identity remains intact in spite of transposition.
6   Schuller, *Early Jazz*, p. 78.
7   See Frank Tirro, "The Silent Theme Tradition in Jazz," *Musical Quarterly* 53 (1967), 324.
8   Schuller, *Early Jazz*, p. 134.
9   In a lecture given in 1957, Gunther Schuller coined this term for a kind of music in which elements of jazz and European fine-art music were intentionally combined. Since that time the phrase has become the accepted designation for such music. See Chapter 6 for a discussion of this development.

Color and Instrumentation

Until approximately 1960 the performance of jazz had been confined to a relatively small number of European instruments. They included the trumpet, the trombone, the clarinet, the saxophone, the piano, the tuba, the string bass, the guitar, the drums, and the voice. During this time a smaller number of secondary instruments, such as the violin, the flute, the vibraharp, and the French horn, also appeared as exceptions to standard instrumentation, usually in connection with an especially talented performer or an arranger. Coloristic variety was produced within this narrow range by contrasting instrumental families against each other and by using a vocabulary of timbral effects exclusive to jazz performance practice. The emphasis on color during the vogue of the cool style in the fifties might be seen as a preliminary effort to the widespread acceptance of new instruments that took place in jazz after 1960.

In the jazz produced after 1960, color became a consideration of greater importance than it had ever been in the past. This becomes evident by means of an accounting of the unprecedented assortment of instrumental resources and coloristic effects found in the jazz of this period. Musical color in jazz has been enriched by the use of exotic instruments from non-Western musical traditions, the use of African concepts of tone production and vocal practice, the acceptance of all European instruments, the use of procedures adopted from the fine-art music avant-garde, the use of electronic or electronically modified instruments, and the use of new orchestrational combinations.

THE TURN TO AFRICA FOR NEW COLOR

The awareness of non-Western musical cultures by American jazz musicians was not a purely musical development. Extra-musical, sociological factors were of extreme importance to the jazz musician's investigation of exotic instruments and practices. Because of the new-found solidarity among blacks in America during the sixties and the newly defined alienation from White America resulting from it, American blacks began to look to the Third World — to Africa, Asia, and South America — with new interest. Africa was, of course, the primary interest.

As a result of this cultural climate, many blacks abandoned Christianity and embraced the Islamic faith of the Black Muslims. The Black Muslim movement, initiated in the United States by W. D. Fard in 1930, enjoyed a certain popularity in the forties, but commanded national attention in the sixties. The attraction of a number of jazz musicians to Islam was soon followed by a fascination for the music of the Islamic world, Northern Africa and Arabia. Musicians such as Yusef Lateef, Ornette Coleman, John Coltrane, Randy Weston, Herbie Mann, Art Blakey, Rahsaan Roland Kirk, and Sahib Shihab gave expression to their North African interest in jazz composition and improvisation. In spite of the employment of ethnic scales and appropriately nasal tone production, the relationship of these Arabian-inspired works remained for the most part evocative and indirect.

Use of African Instruments

Many black musicians turned to Africa, their once-denied roots, for new sources of instrumental color. The more conspicuous were those black jazz artists who associated themselves with the militant social movement that rejected the long sought assimilation of blacks into the mainstream of American society and espoused a "separate but equal" doctrine for the two races. These musicians, who became known collectively as Black Nationalist musicians, perceived their music as a form of protest and intentionally devalued the European aspects of their art. Other black jazz musicians who were empathetic but not as socially militant as their Black Nationalist colleagues were likewise attracted to the new possibilities suggested by African musical practice.

The most obvious reference to African music was the introduction of African instruments into jazz performance situations. Reed and wooden flutes and whistles of various sizes, the thumb piano (the *sansa*), horns fashioned from animal horns, and a variety of bells, rattles, and drums were among the new additions. The conga drum, a Caribbean version of the African drum, was frequently added to the instrumentation of small groups. These African instruments were usually employed in an accompanimental manner, providing additional layers of sonority to support melodic improvisation.

This imitation of complex African rhythmic textures was also manifested in the use of more than one drummer in the jazz ensemble. The presence of two drummers, each in command of a standard jazz drum set, became common. Examples of this practice are *Meditations* by John Coltrane (Impulse AS–9110, 1966) and *Live-Evil* by Miles Davis (Columbia G–30954, 1970). The use of two quartets, each with its own drummer, by Ornette Coleman for his recording *Free Jazz* (Atlantic 1364, 1960), although it was not an acknowledged African reference, suggests similar artistic goals. The augmentation of the jazz ensemble by means of percussion instruments enabled performers to create layers of polyrhythmic-polymetric activity and to produce a new level of rhythmic density in their music.

The Appearance of "Melodic" Drumming

There also appeared a new approach to jazz drumming, a melodic one reminiscent of a fundamental principle of African drumming. A consideration of pitch in drumming practice, an obvious aspect of the drum languages of African tribal communication, has by no means reached its equal in sophistication in American jazz drumming, nor is this likely. The tendency for jazz drummers, however, to make pitch contributions, to create melodically interesting patterns of percussion sounds, became common practice in the sixties. The use of the tom-tom during the Swing Era was certainly pitch-oriented and may be an earlier manifestation of similar goals.

The emergence of this type of drumming in the sixties was a parallel development to the disappearance of the traditional rhythm section in some quarters of jazz activity. In the movement toward collective expression and collective improvisation, the assignment of somewhat rigid roles to the various members of the combo had become obsolete as each member became responsible for "keeping time" and supplying harmony. The assumption of new responsibilities by the solo improvisers liberated not only the drummer, but the other members of the rhythm section as well. The development of this drumming concept can be traced in the playing of Kenny Clarke, Max Roach, Dannie Richmond, Elvin Jones, and Tony Williams.

Pitch-oriented drumming appeared in the sixties immediately prior to the acceptance of rock drumming patterns into the jazz idiom and was, in a certain sense, compatible with the rock drumming style. Rock drumming requires a definition of tone capable of competing with the precise attacks of the electric guitar and electric bass. Pitch elements are often integral features of rock ostinato patterns.

The Imitation of African Concepts of Tone Quality

Another development that can be seen as an African influence was the desire to produce more primitive-sounding effects on standard instruments, especially the reeds. Not only was this considered to be an imitation of African concepts of tone production and melodic inflection by its proponents, but it was boldly crude in its rejection of European concepts of tone production and beauty. Melodic imitation of speech inflection is an essential factor in African music because of Africa's "tonal" languages, speech systems in which word meaning is dependent upon the pitch of each syllable of the word. To preserve word meaning, African melodies must conform in their general contour to the spoken word.

The vital relationship between melodic inflection and the spoken word, a decisive factor to the very nature of African melody, has long been recognized as a characteristic of the music of the Afro-American. Its emphatic reappearance in the sixties was indicative of the new black pride and a glorification of the black heritage.

> These young musicians . . . rely to a great extent on a closeness of vocal reference. . . . Players like Coleman, Coltrane, and Rollins literally scream and rant in imitation of the human voice, sounding many times like the unfettered primitive shouter. Charlie Parker also had to restore this quality of jazz timbre after the legitimizing of commercial swing.[1]

The roughness, the urgency, the edge — the naturalness — of the playing of Ornette Coleman, John Coltrane, and Sonny

Rollins (all saxophonists) had a profound effect on the wood-wind sound of the sixties. Their conception of tone quality was the point of departure for many jazz musicians, most notably Black Nationalist jazz musicians. The exploitation of supposedly African-like sounds, a new vocabulary of electrifying growls and moans for melodic purposes, was a fundamental mannerism of the music of militant blacks and certainly symbolic of their social protest. The similarity of these practices to the extension of expressive devices on conventional instruments in the avant-garde of the European tradition is to be observed. Examples of these practices can be heard on the recording *New Wave in Jazz* (Impulse A–90, 1965) and on recordings by saxophonists Albert Ayler, Archie Shepp, and Pharoah Sanders as well as those by Coleman, Coltrane, and Rollins.

There was also imitation of African singing techniques. African-inspired singing, chanting, and yelling were introduced into the jazz experience. By the early seventies there were more serious efforts to approximate African singing. Leon Thomas adopted a vocal style from Southwest Africa, a kind of yodelling known as *mokambi*. This can be heard on his album *Spirits Known and Unknown* (Flying Dutchman 10115, 1974).

Performance with African Musicians

The American jazz musicians' exposure to authentic African music was actually quite limited. A small number of recordings of African music were in existence, but generally unavailable. Ethnomusicological analyses had produced only limited understanding of African musical customs and, in any event, were circulated primarily among a small group of European and American scholars. During the period in question, however, important achievements in African music scholarship, such as *Studies in African Music* by A. M. Jones (London: Oxford University Press, 1959), appeared, and the number of recordings of African music increased substantially. The impact of ethnomusicological scholarship and recordings on jazz musicians has not been documented. It is known, for example, that Eric Dolphy acknowledged the singing of African pygmies as an influence to his playing.[2]

A desire for more practical instruction in African music

resulted in a number of musical pilgrimages to Africa by prominent jazz musicians. Not only did these occasions provide first-
hand experience with the music and its instruments, but they
also presented to American jazz artists the opportunity to perform with native musicians. There was little attempt at synthesiz-
ing the two traditions. The outcome was rather a combination of
the two, usually in the form of jazz improvisation supported by a
dense foundation of African rhythms. Recorded examples of
such musical confrontations include *Live at the Pan-African Festival* by Archie Shepp (Actuel 51, 1969), *Jazz Meets Arabia: Noon in
Tunisia* by Jean-Luc Ponty and Sahib Shihab (BASF/MPS ST–
20640, 1966), and *Plays with the Master Musicians of Joujouka,
Morocco* by Ornette Coleman. Pianist and composer Randy Weston, after several visits to Africa, moved there for an extended
period in the later part of the decade and continued to produce
jazz with more authentic African elements.

Earlier John Coltrane, who had exhibited a strong interest
in African drumming, had befriended Michael Babaunde
Olatunji, a Nigerian percussionist and teacher living in New
York. Olatunji was the leader of a drum ensemble and the found-
er of the Olatunji Center of African Culture in Harlem. Although the drummer did perform with other jazz musicians,
Coltrane and his Nigerian friend never performed together.
The appearance of an African drummer in an American jazz
ensemble was not at all unusual by the end of the decade.

THE TURN TO ASIA FOR NEW COLOR

As many blacks were turning to Africa for new sounds,
others — blacks and whites — were attracted to the musical
cultures of Asia. American interest in Asian musical resources
and in the tradition from which they spring was related to the
spiritual connotation Oriental music possesses. The distinctive,
non-Western sounds of these instruments, their hypnotic and
exotic timbres, satisfied the romantic requirements of American
ears for new color.

The "Classical Music" of India

A focal point of interest for American jazz musicians in this
regard was the *rāga*, the "classical music" of India. The central

figure in transmitting Indian musical practice and its underlying philosophical system to American jazz musicians and jazz audiences was the Indian *sitār* master Ravi Shankar. Before leaving the Los Angeles area in the spring of 1965, at the close of his term as artist-in-residence at the University of California, Los Angeles, Shankar and his ensemble presented a farewell concert at one of the more prestigious jazz clubs on the West Coast at that time, Shelly's Manne-Hole in Hollywood. In 1968 Shankar won second place in the best-musician-of-the-year category of the *down beat* Reader's Poll, the first musician from a non-Western musical tradition to be honored so. It is reported that Shankar and John Coltrane exchanged letters as a result of the latter's investigation of Indian music. Coltrane's correspondence with Shankar began in 1961 and was culminated by their first meeting in November 1965.[3] Wind players Yusef Lateef, who became especially well-known for his use of Asian and Near Eastern materials,[4] and Eric Dolphy, who became influential in the avant-garde before his unexpected death in 1964,[5] also acknowledged conversations with Shankar as high points in their own informal educations in Indian music.

Paul Horn, jazz flutist, was also directly associated with Shankar.[6] It was Horn who introduced Shankar to many prominent Los Angeles musicians when the Indian musician visited that city in 1964. Shankar chose Horn to perform on his recording *Portrait of Genius* (World Pacific WPS–1432, 1965) and supervised Horn's first practical experience with Indian music for the purposes of that recording. Horn's friendship with Shankar changed the direction of the jazz artist's career and was responsible for his new spiritual orientation. Soon after that recording, Horn began a course of study in the elements of Indian music with Shankar's colleague Hari Har Rao, the teacher of Indian music in the UCLA department of ethnomusicology. Horn became known for his attempts to imitate the sound of the classical bamboo flute of India on its European counterpart.

In spite of the teaching efforts of Shankar and their sincere reception by jazz musicians, Shankar was not a party to any contrived synthesis of Indian music and jazz. He was primarily concerned with transmitting the essence of Indian music and was quick to distinguish the differences between the two musics.[7]

Interviews with Shankar and accounts of his performances appeared with some regularity in jazz-oriented periodicals during the second half of the sixties.

The Use of Indian Instruments

The association of trumpet player Don Ellis with Hari Har Rao resulted in the formation of the Hindustani Jazz Sextet. This group, which flourished around 1965, was an effort to find common ground between jazz and the music of India. Its instrumentation included *sitār, dhōlaka, tabla,* trumpet, alto saxophone, tenor saxophone, organ, string bass, and drums.

Ellis's attempts to fuse jazz and Indian music represent, perhaps, the most conspicuous use of Indian instruments in the jazz of the sixties. In other situations these instruments were employed as coloristic additions to standard jazz ensembles. Indian instruments which appeared in the jazz of this period included the following:

sānāyī:	conical shawm of Northern India, made of wood, often with metal bell.
sitār:	long-necked lute of gourd or teakwood with movable frets beneath four to seven metal strings; usually found with additional resonating strings; plucked with wire plectrum.
tamburā:	drone lute similar to the sitār; body of wood or gourd with long unfretted neck and four metal strings; plucked with fingers.
tabla:	small drum with body of wood, metal, or clay, with single head; generally played in conjunction with another drum, the bāmyā.
bāmyā:	small indoor kettledrum with body of clay, wood, or metal; played exclusively with the tabla.
mridanga:	elongated drum with heads of unequal diameter; hollowed from a single block of wood; played with wrists and fingertips.
dhōlaka:	barrel-shaped drum with heads of identical diameter; shell hollowed from single block of wood.

To compete with the increased dynamic range of electronic instruments that was characteristic of jazz in the latter half of the decade, electronic alterations, especially electronic amplification, were made on adopted Indian instruments. At the end of the decade, for example, Miles Davis included an electric *sitār* in his ensemble.

The popularity of Indian instruments and the influence of Indian music on jazz in general reached their highest levels following the well-publicized flirtation with Indian music by the Beatles in the mid-sixties and the great public success of Shankar at that time. There had been, however, serious experimentation with Indian musical resources before these events. These developments reflect a general cultural climate in which non-Western elements were matters of fascination.

The use of Indian instruments in jazz performance situations can be heard on the following representative recordings: *Electric Bath* by Don Ellis (Columbia CS-9585, 1968), *Journey in Satchidananda* by Alice Coltrane (Impulse AS 9203, 1970), and *Big Fun* by Miles Davis (Columbia PG–32866, 1969/70/72).

The Use of Other Asian Instruments

A number of other Asian instruments, typically those for which long periods of instruction were unnecessary, were also introduced into jazz. Oriental flutes and percussion instruments, such as bells, gongs, and drums, appeared. The Japanese *koto* appeared on recordings by the Art Ensemble of Chicago.

THE TURN TO SOUTH AMERICA FOR NEW COLOR

The Use of Brazilian Instruments

The popularity of the *bossa nova* in the early sixties and its adaptation by American jazz musicians brought considerable attention to the musical customs of Brazil. In an effort to capture the true character of the *bossa nova,* American musicians adopted an assortment of Afro-Brazilian percussion instruments. A similar borrowing of Latin American percussion instruments had accompanied an Afro-Cuban fad in the late forties and early fifties. Brazilian instruments[8] most commonly employed within a jazz context included the following:

agogó: metal hand bell struck with metal rod.

atabaque: elongated drum with one head; identified by Sinzig as a variant of the square drum.

berimbao: musical bow whose string is passed through a gourd resonator; gourd held to player's chest, string stopped by fingers and struck with a stick or nail (urucungo).

cabaça: gourd rattle covered with a network of shells or beads.

chocalho: shaker or rattle similar to cabaça.

cuíca: friction drum with friction stick, rubbed with wetted hand or cloth; capable of producing different pitches.

frigideira: metal frying pan struck with metal rod.

ganzá: rattle in the shape of a closed cylinder, made of tin plate.

pandeiro: tambourine.

réco-réco: notched bamboo or metal segment scraped with a piece of bamboo.

surdo: muted drum, usually a tamborim (see next item).

tamborim: small one-headed drum consisting of a half barrel, held under the arm and struck with the opposing hand.

zabumba: family of drums existing in various sizes; the tenor and bass drums are most common.

Performance with Brazilian Musicians

As a result of the *bossa nova,* American jazz and Brazilian popular music experienced a mutual exchange of musicians: Americans travelled to Brazil to hear and perform with native musicians, and Brazilian musicians were well-received within American performing and recording circles. The former case is exemplified by the recordings *The Sound of Ipanema* (Columbia CS–9072, 1964) and *Rio* (Columbia CS–9115, 1965) by alto saxophonist Paul Winter and *Do the Bossa Nova* by flutist Herbie Mann (Atlantic 1397, 1963). The Winter albums represent collaborations between the American alto saxophonist and Carlos Lyra, Luiz Bonfá, Roberto Menescal, and Luiz Eça, composer-performers of the popular Brazilian music. For his recording, Mann joined forces with "Zézinho e sua Escola de Samba," a seventeen-piece percussion ensemble comprised of the leading Brazilian "school of samba" musicians. Musical organizations such as this one were typical of the groups that perform in the streets of Rio de Janeiro during the Carnival. On the other hand, such notable Brazilian musicians as António Carlos Jobim, João Gilberto, Lalo Schifrin, Sérgio Mendes, and later Airto Moreira enjoyed great success in the United States as proponents of Brazilian-influenced jazz.

THE TURN TO EUROPEAN FINE-ART MUSIC FOR NEW COLOR

Acceptance of More European Instruments

As the color spectrum of jazz was being enhanced by the addition of instruments from the Third World, a similar development was taking place with respect to European instruments. This reappraisal of European instrumental resources resulted in the playing of jazz on traditionally non-jazz European instruments or on instruments that had disappeared from jazz performance. There was obviously a strong relationship between this development and the practical intentions of third-stream proponents, although the use of such instruments was by no means confined to jazz musicians associated with that movement.

There was virtually a renaissance of interest in the soprano saxophone due to the leadership role provided by the highly influential John Coltrane. Berendt has suggested that the popularity of the soprano saxophone was partially related to the jazz musician's ability to approximate the sound of the *zoukra,* an oboe-like instrument of the Middle East. Miles Davis was similarly responsible for the popularity of the *Flügelhorn*, although his interest predated 1960. The flute, with the aid of electronic amplification, became universally accepted. The violin, the cello, the oboe, the bassoon, the celeste, and the harp were given places in jazz largely because of the freshness of their respective timbres. The clarinet and the tuba, once prominent and characteristic jazz instruments, reappeared. Additions to the timbral palette made by cool era musicians, such as the French horn, the alto flute, the bass trombone, and the *Flügelhorn*, were retained. The entire range of standard percussion instruments —

the complement of any twentieth-century symphony orchestra — became the common property of jazz musicians. The performance of jazz on historical European instruments, such as the harpsichord and the recorder, also occurred.

The importance of such timbral considerations is strengthened by the emergence of virtuoso jazz performers on the "new" instruments. A representative list might include Jean-Luc Ponty, violin; Hubert Laws, flute; Howard Johnson, tuba; Eric Dolphy, bass clarinet; Yusef Lateef, oboe; and Dorothy Ashby, harp.

The Expansion of the Sound Vocabulary of Instruments

During the sixties jazz artists displayed an interest in increasing the sound vocabulary of traditional instruments. This was achieved by expanding the normal ranges of wind instruments and by exploring unconventional means of tone production. The use of harmonics and false tones became common. Once-unorthodox procedures such as manually plucking, stroking, and hammering the strings of a piano; singing, grunting, and screaming through wind instruments; the simultaneous playing and singing through wind instruments; rattling sticks inside of a piano; and singing into a drumhead to make it vibrate became acceptable.

The use of the voice was subjected to similar types of experimentation. In the *We Insist: Freedom Now Suite* (Candid 8002, 1960) composed by drummer Max Roach, one movement, entitled "The Protest," consists of several minutes of unaccompanied screaming by vocalist Abbey Lincoln. In *A Love Supreme* (Impulse S–77, 1964), members of John Coltrane's ensemble contributed to the musical texture by chanting a repeated motive in unison. A form of melodrama, spoken recitation with jazz accompaniment, can be found in Archie Shepp's tribute to Malcolm X "Malcolm, Malcolm — Semper Malcolm" on the recording *Fire Music* (Impulse AS–86, 1965) and in the readings by Black Nationalist poet LeRoi Jones accompanied by the music of John Tchicai. Vocalist Fontella Bass employed a type of speech-singing in her performances with the Art Ensemble of Chicago, such as *Les Stances a Sophie* (Nessa N–4, 1970). Yusef Lateef exploited an unusual vocal effect by his use of an animal horn:

> Perhaps the most intriguing instance of extemporization is
> Lateef's striking sub-vocalization, in which the human voice
> is projected through the opening at the large end of a cow's
> horn. . . . This device is further modified by inserting the
> horn into the resonating holes [*sic*] in the piano, setting in
> motion a complex series of harmonics as the neighboring
> strings vibrate sympathetically.[10]

The importance of the voice, especially its flexibility and its wide
range of possible sounds, was also manifested in the imitation of
vocal practice by instrumentalists.

The adoption of these kinds of instrumental and vocal
techniques by jazz musicians reflects the influence of the avant-
garde of Western fine-art music. Their use in jazz was frequently, but not exclusively, associated with what was considered
the avant-garde movement in jazz during the early years of the
sixties.

THE USE OF ELECTRONIC INSTRUMENTS

Perhaps the most fundamental change with respect to musical color in the jazz of the sixties was the acceptance of electronic
instruments into jazz performance practice in the last years of
the decade. In this context "electronic instruments" is used as a
generic term for those instruments in which the tone is amplified, modified, or produced electronically. The popularization of many devices developed in electronic studios and ultimately adopted by jazz musicians, however, first occurred in the
realm of rock and roll.

In spite of the general influence of rock instrumental practice on the use of electronic instruments in jazz, Berendt has
documented the initial experimentation with several electronic
innovations as the work of jazz musicians prior to their acceptance into rock and roll: the electric guitar by Charlie Christian in
1939; the electric organ in black rhythm-and-blues combos,
championed by Jimmy Smith after 1956; the electric piano by
Ray Charles in 1959, brought to renewed prominence by Miles
Davis's sidemen Herbie Hancock and Chick Corea in 1968; and
the first experimentation with electronically amplified and modified wind instruments by Sonny Stitt in 1966 and Lee Konitz in
1968.[11] Sun Ra[12] was also using the electric piano in the late
fifties.

Electronic Amplification of Sound

In the electronization of traditional instruments, the tone is generated by conventional means, such as reeds or strings, and amplified by electronic means. This is done by mounting a small microphone in the airstream of wind instruments (flute, saxophone, trumpet, trombone) or by converting string vibrations directly into electrical signals (electric bass, electric guitar, electric violin). The obvious advantage to the use of these instruments is their greater capability for volume and projection. The original sound of an instrument, moreover, is slightly changed because the way the sound has been produced has also been amplified. For this reason articulation becomes prominent.

Electronic Modification of Sound

In addition to the simple amplification of sound, the use of electronic equipment has enabled the performer to alter the tone itself.[13] This is achieved by modifying the harmonic organization of the tone, by omitting or reconstituting specific overtones that make up the original sound. With an octave divider, also known as the multivider, the given pitch may be doubled one octave lower. With some sophisticated versions of this device, the original pitch may be omitted or transposed two octaves lower or one octave higher. The octave divider may also be used to simulate the timbres of other standard instruments, such as the cello, the bassoon, and the tuba. The varitone, a device similar to the octave divider, permits the automatic harmonization of melodic lines at designated intervals.

The sound envelope of a given pitch — its attack and decay characteristics — may also be subjected to electronic manipulation. The use of reverberation units, wah-wah pedals, fuzz tone pedals, phase shifters, and various sound filters greatly increases the number of coloristic options available to the performer. An echo device, the echoplex, has become especially attractive to the jazz soloist, who is enabled by its use to superimpose new material on an electronically produced "echo" of his own solo. A performer is thus capable of creating a contrapuntal texture by himself.

The echo device, essentially a tape loop receiving sound from a recording head then feeding that sound immediately into one or more playback heads as it moves past them, makes possible instant tone-repetition. And since the playback heads can be fed back into the recording head, complex patterns of sound-repetition can be built, even from a single note. Furthermore, when the initial portion of the tape again reaches the recording head, sound on sound becomes still another of this machine's effective uses.[14]

An early example of the echo device in an improvised solo can be heard in a trumpet solo by Don Ellis in his composition "Open Beauty" from his album *Electric Bath* (Columbia CS–9585, 1968).

When electronic modifications become available because of an attachment to an otherwise traditional instrument, that instrument retains its ability to produce natural sounds as another option.

Prominent jazz performers who adopted electronic instruments included the following: Miles Davis, Don Ellis, the electric trumpet; Chick Corea, Herbie Hancock, the electric piano; John McLaughlin, the electric guitar; Jean-Luc Ponty, Jerry Goodman, the electric violin; Sonny Stitt, Lee Konitz, the electric saxophone; and Hubert Laws, Paul Horn, the electric flute.

The Use of the Synthesizer

Finally there are two common electronic instruments that use electronic tone generators: the electronic organ, especially the Hammond organ which had become the mainstay of black rhythm-and-blues in the fifties, and the synthesizer, especially the portable transistorized keyboard models developed by R. A. Moog, Donald Buchla, and Tonus, Inc. (the Arp) after 1965. Experimentation with the musical possibilities of the synthesizer had begun in the mid-fifties and had been carried on by such respected fine-art composers as Vladimir Ussachevsky, Otto Luening, and Milton Babbitt since the early sixties, but any similar interest in the synthesizer by popular and jazz musicians at that time would have been not only economically impractical, but aesthetically inconceivable. It was not until 1968, when Walter Carlos employed the Moog synthesizer to simulate traditional instruments in his recording of several compositions by Johann Sebastian Bach (*Switched-on Bach,* Columbia MS–7194, 1968), that the synthesizer became widely known to the general music public. By this time the Moog synthesizer had become economically feasible and attracted a small number of jazz as well as rock musicians.

Paul Bley, Sun Ra, and Herbie Hancock were notable early experimenters with the synthesizer in the jazz idiom. Its treatment in general was restricted to that of a novel keyboard instrument, one mostly confined to the simulation of known sounds or the production of superficial sound effects. The exploration of new sounds and new instrumental possibilities was a gradual process. By the end of the sixties, the potential of the synthesizer as a source of all sound had barely been realized. In spite of the increasing use of the synthesizer in jazz, its adaptation as a legitimate jazz instrument remained even into the seventies in the experimental stage. The performance on the Moog synthesizer by Herb Deutsch and Chris Swanson in the final concert of the Museum of Modern Art's 1969 "Jazz in the Garden" series, however, was a landmark of sorts in that it marked one of the first appearances of the Moog synthesizer as a "live performance" instrument.[15]

The exception to the rather unimaginative use of the synthesizer for improvisation in this early period was Sun Ra, who was apparently the most adept in exploiting the synthesizer's inherent potential for continuous variation of all sound parameters. The most instructive example of his work is the extended solo in "Cosmic Explorer" on his album *Nuits de la Fondation Maeght,* Vol. I (Shandar SR–10.001, 1970).

The Use of Tape Music

The use of tape music, either electronically modified "natural" sounds or electronically generated sounds, appears to have been of little interest to jazz musicians. The absence of any degree of spontaneity in the preparation and performance of such musical resources may have been an inhibiting factor. There was, however, at least one such experiment. The performance of a work entitled *Imperfections in a Given Space,* a collaboration of a jazz quartet led by Joseph Jarman and tape music prepared and executed by John Cage, was reported to have taken place in late 1965.[16]

THE USE OF NEW ORCHESTRATIONAL COMBINATIONS

The Big Band

The addition of new instruments to jazz ensembles forced the performers, their arrangers, and their composers to re-evaluate orchestrational procedures. For this reason, the sixties became a period of orchestrational experimentation. This was especially the case with respect to the larger jazz ensembles, groups in which the number of untried possibilities was particularly large. Stereotyped orchestration had been an important distinguishing factor in earlier jazz styles. The sound so characteristic of the Swing Era big band, for example, was the result of the homogeneous combination of instruments arranged in a specific manner, with each section acting as a unit. This type of orchestrational uniformity was not a stylistic trait of large ensemble jazz in the sixties.

By the late fifties, the big band was already suffering from cliché-ridden instrumental resources and treatments. The choice of different combinations of instruments for the doubling of unison melodic lines and for playing harmonized ensemble passages and the tendency toward more independent part-writing within instrumental sections had an invigorating effect on that medium. The traditional five-member reed section consisted of 2 alto saxophones, 2 tenor saxophones, and 1 baritone saxophone. Occasionally members would double on clarinet or flute. The five-member reed section of Don Ellis's big band, as heard on his recording *Electric Bath* (Columbia CS–9585, 1968), included 1 piccolo, 5 flutes, 2 clarinets, 1 bass clarinet, 2 soprano saxophones, 2 alto saxophones, 2 tenor saxophones, and 1 baritone saxophone. The number of orchestrational permutations possible in the latter instance is unquestionably larger and is the basis for a much higher level of orchestrational diversity. The 1968 Ellis reed section is presented only as one example. Although the saxophone, trumpet, and trombone continued to be the nucleus of the big band, instrumentation was by no means standard and differed from one composition to another.

As must be inferred from the preceding discussion, the practice of doubling on a number of instruments became an even more important responsibility for jazz musicians in the six-

31

ties than ever before. For example, all members of Sun Ra's big band performed on secondary instruments, often traditional or African percussion instruments. In the same spirit, their leader surrounded himself with a sizable battery of keyboard instruments: the piano, the electric piano, the organ, and the synthesizer.

By modifying inherited organization and instrumentation, the big band of the sixties became a kaleidoscope of instrumental color. Examples of achievement in this sphere of activity are *The Black Saint and the Sinner Lady* by Charles Mingus (Impulse AS–35, 1963); *Electric Bath* by Don Ellis (Columbia CS–9585, 1968); *The Heliocentric World of Sun Ra,* Vol. I, by Sun Ra (ESP–1014, 1965); and *Central Park North* by Thad Jones and Mel Lewis (Solid State 18058, 1969).

Other Large Jazz Ensembles

Large jazz ensembles which did not use the traditional big-band format as a point of departure were formed during the sixties. Musical examples of this development are the various recordings made under the auspices of the Association for the Advancement of Creative Musicians, a Chicago-based jazz collective formed in 1965. The music of its members was fashioned according to the precepts of "free jazz." The matters of tone color and unconventional orchestration were extremely important to their over-all conception. The quantity and variety of their instrumental resources far exceeded comparison with contemporary groups. These included slide whistles, police whistles, recorders, the harp, the Japanese *koto*, the kazoo, the harmonica, a thunder sheet, bells and gongs, and many other percussion instruments. The use of such "sound makers" was considered to be neither incidental, nor a manifestation of gimmickry or novelty for its own sake. These sounds were well integrated into the rather distinctive fabric of the music produced by this "school" of jazz musicians.

Another extraordinary feature of the music of this group is the periodic presence of static sound blocks, the accumulation of sustained pitches without rhythmic motion or rhythmic articulation. These sound masses are subjected to gradual changes in pitch content, instrumental shading, and dynamics. In spite of the harmonic vagueness of these passages, the maintenance of a pedal point in the bass usually acts as a reference to a tonal center. The impression of vagueness is compounded by the accompaniment of percussion instruments of appropriately indefinite articulation, such as gongs, bells, and rattles. The absence of articulation and motion is enhanced by the lack of intensity by which the sound surfaces were created in apparently both improvised and calculated circumstances. The musical emphasis is obviously on timbre. The source of this procedure is, of course, contemporary fine-art music. Recorded examples may be heard on *Levels and Degrees of Light* by Richard Abrams (Delmark 413, 1968) and *Song For* by Joseph Jarman (Delmark 410, 1967).

The Combo

This type of coloristic experimentation was not uncommon in the music of post-1960 small-group jazz. The use of new instrumental mixtures increased the number of options for combo soloists. For example, in his 1965 combo performances, Yusef Lateef personally played the flute, the tenor saxophone, the oboe, an assortment of wooden flutes, the sānāyī, a scraper of animal horn, a small brass hand bell, and the tambourine.[17] His competence in exploiting diverse instrumentation may be heard on *1984* (Impulse A–84, 1966), in which his resources included flutes (Taiwan, Chinese wind, Czech, MaMa, cork), bells (tubular, Chinese, Indian), triangle, celeste, cow's horn, tambourine, tenor saxophone, and oboe. Likewise, Ornette Coleman displayed remarkable versatility by performing on such contrasting instruments as the saxophone, the trumpet, and the violin.

THE RAMIFICATION OF THE SEARCH FOR COLOR

The acceptance of new sound resources by the jazz musicians of the sixties was in effect a manifestation of a reaching out for different or more intense musical stimuli. It is unnecessary to list further the many instruments used to create jazz at that time. The fact is that, although standard instruments remained important, jazz musicians felt free to make music by any means they chose. Their spirit of experimentation with sound and color was a by-product of a need to communicate on their own terms. In doing so, they developed a new type of jazz in which sound was no longer always the means but an end in itself: sound for the sake of sensuous sound.

This attitude was the gift of the fine-art avant-garde to the mainstream of music-making. Sound itself is interesting.

> It is quite apparent that in this music [referring to experi-mental music] the composer's chief, if not only concern is the nature of sound itself, whether produced by electronic or conventional means. It thus becomes possible . . . to identify a kind of music that is basically *sound-oriented*, in contrast to that which is more conventionally *theme-oriented*. In one, the sound itself is the significant element, while in the other, the sound is only a vehicle for projecting a the-matic element.[18]

This emphasis on color with its resulting new sense of sonor-ity is surely one of the most significant stylistic characteristics of the jazz produced in the sixties. This is not to imply that theme-oriented jazz did not continue to be created. Yet, even in the music of conservative artists, this concern for color and rich sonority can be heard. The now legendary "sheets of sound" of tenor saxophonist John Coltrane, the "sound pieces" of jazz composer Oliver Nelson, and the "problems of sound" described by jazz avant-garde figure Cecil Taylor were part of the same general musical climate that produced the "sound walls" of Krzysztof Penderecki, the highly-respected contemporary Polish composer of fine-art music.

---

1   LeRoi Jones, *Blues People* (New York: Morrow, 1963), p. 227.
2   Robert Levin, record liner notes to *Eric Dolphy in Europe*, vol. 1 (Prestige PR–7304, 1963).
3   This correspondence is mentioned briefly in Richard Turner, "John Coltrane: A Biographical Sketch," *Black Perspective in Music* 3 (Spring 1975), 9; and J. C. Thomas, *Chasin' the Trane: The Music and Mystique of John Coltrane* (Garden City, N.Y.: Doubleday, 1975), p. 200.
4   Pete Welding, "Music as Color: Yusef Lateef," *down beat* 32 (May 20, 1965), 22.
5   Vladimir Simosko & Barry Tepperman, *Eric Dolphy: A Musical Biog-raphy and Discography* (Washington, D.C.: Smithsonian Institution Press, 1974), p. 13.

6   Robert Palmer, record liner notes to *Paul Horn in India* by Paul Horn and native Indian instrumentalists (Blue Note LA529–H2, reissued 1975).

7   John A. Tynan, "India's Master Musician: Ravi Shankar," *down beat* 32 (May 6, 1965), 16.

8   The primary source for this information was Marcuse, *Musical Instruments.* Supplementary information was taken from Frei Pedro Sinzig, *Dicionário musical,* 2d ed. (Rio de Janeiro: Livraria Kosmos Editora, 1959); Oneyda Alvarenga, *Música popular brasileña* (Buenos Aires: Fondo de Cultura Económica, 1947); Gerard Béhague, "Bossa & Bossas: Recent Changes in Brazilian Urban Popular Music," *Ethnomusicology* 17 (1973), 209–33; and John K. Galm, "How to Perk Up Percussion," *down beat* 42 (December 4, 1975), 36–37.

9   Joachim-Ernst Berendt, *The Jazz Book,* trans. by Dan Morgenstern, Helmut Bredigkeit, and Barbara Bredigkeit (New York: Lawrence Hill, 1975), p. 106.

10   Robert Hammer, record liner notes to *1984* by Yusef Lateef (Impulse S–84, 1966).

11   Berendt, *The Jazz Book,* p. 44.

12   Sun Ra is the pseudonym assumed in the mid-fifties by pianist Herman Sonny Blount (born ca. 1910). Since that time he has surrounded his experimental jazz with elements of mythology and mysticism and has adopted a multi-media performance style. His big band is known as the "Arkestra."

13   See the annotated list of electronic devices used by jazz musicians in William L. Fowler, "How to Electrify a Horn and an Audience," *down beat* 41 (July 18, 1974), 42. (Reprinted with permission of *down beat.*)

14   Fowler, "How to Electrify," 42.

15   Thomas LeMar Rhea, "The Evolution of Electronic Musical Instruments in the United States," Ph.D. dissertation, George Peabody College for Teachers, 1972, p. 211.

16   Pete Welding, "Caught in the Act: Joseph Jarman — John Cage," *down beat* 33 (January 13, 1966), 35.

17   Welding, "Music as Color: Yusef Lateef," 20.

18   Wayne Barlow, "Electronic Music: Challenge to Music Education," *Music Educators Journal* 55 (November 1968), 68.

Texture and Volume

The concern for color exhibited in jazz produced after 1960 was closely related to the development of new levels of textural density. Jazz musicians of the period manipulated newly-acquired sounds and techniques to complicate the texture of their music. The transparency of previous jazz styles disappeared as the sixties passed. In earlier times big-band music had been arranged in such a way that passages for the several instrumental sections were well delineated. In the combo music of the forties and fifties, each instrumental line was distinctive and distinguishable.

During the sixties many jazz musicians intentionally sought to obscure this inherited sense of order. In their struggle to free themselves from traditional procedures, they focused their attention on creating an over-all effect by means of their music and, in the process, subordinated their concern for musical details. It was as if the individual part had importance only in relationship to its contribution to the whole. The actual pitches were often not significant, which was exactly the contention of many Black Nationalist jazz musicians: "It's not about notes any more, it's about feelings."[1] The density and complexity of texture and the effect produced — the summation of sound — were valuable musical ends in themselves.

The quartet or quintet format that had become idiomatic to concepts of small-group jazz popular before this time was simply an unsuitable vehicle for meeting the dramatic and luxuriant demands created by performers. To produce the desired texture, it became common practice to augment the nuclear combo with more instruments. The added instruments were often assigned relatively simple functions, such as providing a drone, contributing a detail to an ostinato figure, or, in the case of various percussion instruments, adding another layer of rhythmic activity. Such an expansion resulted in the presence of a substantial foundation of sound and rhythmic energy for the support of improvised solos.

VOLUME

The appearance of greater density of texture was accompanied by a correlative demand for greater volume, a prevalent feature of most post-1960 music. Music was to be felt as well as heard. Its listeners were to be enveloped by sound. The presence of more instruments, of course, increased the capacity for a greater range of dynamic levels. Performance practice in general favored louder playing for individual instruments. The intensity made possible by electronic equipment provided the jazz musician with far greater volume potential and with a new sense of power and control. In this context traditional instruments without some form of amplification fell into disuse because of their inability to compete, to cut through the wall of sound for individual display. In many ensembles electronic instruments replaced their "acoustic" equivalents (piano, guitar, string bass).

The increase in volume and the increase in textural density were gradual developments that spanned the decade. In a general sense, the jazz of the sixties was not an intimate music, not an entertainment music, not a background music. The nature of jazz had changed to the extent that, by the end of the decade, it was more at home on the concert stage and with the mass audience than in its former environment, the small jazz club.

ILLUSTRATION OF TEXTURAL DENSITY AND GREATER VOLUME

The capacity of the jazz ensemble for the modification of textural density and for the progressive increase in volume level may be illustrated by examining the instrumentation of selected recordings made under the leadership of Miles Davis between 1959 and 1972. A review of the instrumental forces used by Davis is significant because his music has been among the most respected, most influential, and most progressive in jazz since the early fifties.

Kind of Blue (Columbia CS–8163, 1959)
    trumpet, alto sax, tenor sax, piano, bass, drums

ESP (Columbia CS–9150, 1965)
  trumpet, tenor sax, piano, bass, drums

Miles in the Sky (Columbia CS–9628, 1968)
  trumpet, tenor sax, piano, guitar, bass, drums

In a Silent Way (Columbia CS–9875, 1969)
  trumpet, tenor sax, electric piano (3), organ, guitar, bass,
  drums

Bitches Brew (Columbia 2–GP 26, 1969)
  trumpet, soprano sax, bass clarinet, electric piano (3), electric
  guitar, electric bass, bass, drums (3), accessory percussion

Live-Evil (Columbia G–30954, 1970)
  trumpet, soprano sax, electric keyboards (3), electric guitar,
  electric bass, sitār, voice, drums (2), accessory percussion

Big Fun (Columbia PG–32866, 1969/70/72)
  trumpet, soprano sax, flute, bass clarinet, piano, electric piano
  (2), organ, electric guitar, electric bass, drums (2), African
  percussion, sitār, electric sitār (2), tamboura, tabla

This listing[2] is instructive in that it shows Davis's additions
to the small jazz combo, which began to appear in the latter part
of the decade. His adoption of electronic instruments accompanied his integration of rock elements into his personal jazz
style. Davis himself adopted the electric trumpet. At the end of
the decade, he began to include a variety of coloristically distinctive instruments, such as Indian instruments and African percussion instruments. His use of several instruments of the same
kind, such as three electric pianos and two drum sets, is noteworthy. By 1972 the number of musicians involved in the performance of his music approached the number of instrumentalists
involved in the performance of big-band jazz. Any comparison
of the two types of large jazz ensemble is misleading, however,
because Davis's band was not organized according to instrumental families, but rather maintained a combo orientation with the
added instruments providing a network of rhythmic-harmonic
counterpoint for solo improvisation.

The enrichment of the musical texture and the increase of
dynamic range are major style characteristics of the jazz
produced during the sixties. The process exhibited was an addi-

tive one: more instruments, more instrumental color, more layers of rhythmic activity. Both the vertical and the horizontal aspects of the music were supplemented. In physical terms, there was just more sound — more music — accompanied by a deliberate savoring of its accumulation. There was little use of silence.

Recordings that illustrate these stylistic tendencies include *Free Jazz* by Ornette Coleman (Atlantic 1364, 1960), *Ascension* by John Coltrane (Impulse AS–95, 1965), *Unit Structures* by Cecil Taylor (Blue Note 84237, 1966), *Bitches Brew* by Miles Davis (Columbia 2–GP 26, 1969), and *Live at the Pan-African Festival* by Archie Shepp (Actuel 51, 1969).

---

1   Saxophonist Albert Ayler quoted in Steve Young, record liner notes to *New Wave in Jazz* by various artists (Impulse A–90, 1965).
2   Gregg Hall, "Selected Miles Discography," *down beat* 51 (July 18, 1974), 20, 52; and Bill Cole, *Miles Davis: A Musical Biography* (New York: Morrow, 1974), pp. 170–98.

Melody and Harmony

Traditionally the improvisations of jazz musicians had been governed by the harmonic architecture of a pre-existing piece of music. As each chord in the given harmonic progression was changed, improvisers were obliged also to change the pitch resources stylistically acceptable to be sounded against each specific chord. This was the case whether the improvisation took the form of a melodic paraphrase or that of harmonic variation. This practice has been reduced by jazz theorists and educators[1] to a vocabulary of "chord scales," melodic abstractions from which patterns appropriate for specific chords were chosen.

By the end of the fifties, the challenge of playing the "changes," as the chords are called, became an end in itself. Because of the use of chromatic alterations, the composition of the chords themselves had become more complex. At the same time, the frequency of their appearance within the measure, the harmonic rhythm, had increased. The common practice of chord substitution, the replacement of a structurally important chord with a chord or short progression of similar function, also added to the higher level of complexity.

The harmonic schemes of the three jazz "standards" given as Examples 1–3 exemplify the progressive degrees of complexity to be found in the raw materials for jazz improvisation and typify the nature of the kind of pre-existing compositions rendered in the jazz style. They represent three different periods in the history of jazz: "Muskrat Ramble" (Copyright 1926) by Ray Gilbert and Edward "Kid" Ory, a dixieland favorite; "Georgia on My Mind" (Copyright 1930) by Hoagie Carmichael, a popular song that became a staple in the big-band repertoire; and "'Round Midnight" (ca. 1954) by Thelonius Monk, Cootie Williams, and Bernie Hanigher, a jazz ballad from the fifties that became a classic jazz vehicle. In Example 1 one triad per measure is the norm. The harmonic progression is relatively simple. In Example 2 two chords per measure appear more frequently, and the chords are often colored by the addition of the sixth or seventh degree above the root. In Example 3 three or four chord changes within one measure is not unusual. Chromatic alterations appear with regularity, and the harmonic content has been complicated by the use of chord substitution, most often in the form of secondary dominant chords.

This tradition of improvisation continued throughout the sixties, but not without important attempts at extending or modifying the role of functional harmony and attempts at replacing

Example 1. The Harmonic Scheme of "Muskrat Ramble"

Example 2. The Harmonic Scheme of "Georgia on My Mind"

Example 3. The Harmonic Scheme of "'Round Midnight"

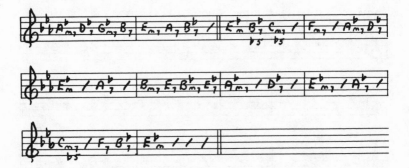

it altogether. This latter development, challenging the necessity of functional harmony to the system of jazz performance, is, perhaps, the single most influential event in the jazz of the sixties. The implications of such a radical approach were extensive and fundamental. It was the first step in a series of creative efforts that ultimately led to "free jazz," a type of jazz in which none of the once-uncontested norms of performance were accepted as obligatory or indispensable.

THE PRESENCE OF A TONAL CENTER

The Introduction of Modal Scales

The first challenge to the traditional use of harmony in jazz appeared in the introduction of modal scales. Like their counterparts in twentieth-century fine-art music, jazz musicians were interested not in the historical use of modal scales "but rather their effectiveness in counter-acting restrictive major-minor conditioning."[2] The use of anachronistic modal scales in both twentieth-century fine-art music and jazz, however, was not a rejection of functional harmony, but an attempt to obscure it without denying the presence of a tonal center. The use of modal scales in twentieth-century fine-art music is characterized by the use of modal scales for melodic construction, the avoidance of the leading tone, unconventional voice-leading, and the use of retrogressive or unorthodox chord progressions.

In jazz the introduction of modal scales served primarily to create a static harmonic situation. Whereas earlier jazz pieces had depended upon chord progression to define key center, modal pieces depended upon the establishment of a drone or pedal point to establish tonal center. The leading tone, the dominant-tonic relationship, and other clichés of traditional harmonic practice were avoided. In earlier jazz pieces, the harmonic content was predetermined; in modal pieces, the vertical element of the music was the result of improvisation.

The advantages of improvising with modal scales centered around the fact that the soloist was no longer responsible for meeting the deadline of the chord changes. In the modal situation an entire solo improvisation could be created by using the pitch resources provided by only one modal scale pattern. The improviser was free to concentrate on melodic, horizontal continuity rather than on a vertically-oriented architecture. And, with the absence of designated chord progressions, it was no longer mandatory to respect the periodicity of eight-, twelve-, and sixteen-measure units, schematic divisions generated by the syntax of functional harmony. The improviser was therefore enabled to exert more control over the structure and length of his solo.

Miles Davis made the following observations about the possibilities offered by modal procedures:

> When you go that way, you can go on forever. You don't have to worry about changes and you can do more with the line. It becomes a challenge to see how melodically inventive you are. When you are based on chords, you know at the end of thirty-two bars that the chords have run out and there's but to repeat what you've just done — with variations. I think that there is a return in jazz to emphasis on melodic rather than harmonic variation. There will be fewer chords but infinite possibilities as to what to do with them. . . . Too much modern jazz has become thick with chords.[3]

"So What," from the album *Kind of Blue* by Miles Davis (Columbia CS–8163, 1959), provides an early and often imitated example of the use of modal scales in jazz. Its monothematic melodic material is cast in traditional thirty-two measure song form, AABA. The melodic idea that appears in each subdivision of the song form is given in Example 4. The Dorian scale is the modal scale assigned to the entire piece with a tonal center of D for the A sections and a shift to E-flat for the B section. The chromatic shift to E-flat for the B section corresponds to the harmonic contrast offered by the "bridge" of the popular song form, but at the same time negates any trace of a functional relationship such as the customary dominant or subdominant. Within the four eight-measure periods, there is no predetermined harmonic movement. The performer is given greater latitude for his improvisation in that repeated choruses result in twenty-four consecutive measures of the D tonal center before an eight-measure digression. The periodicity of the song form, nevertheless, is usually respected in the solo improvisations. The use of the conventional periodic design was a matter of choice or habit, not of inescapable necessity.

Example 4. The Melodic Basis of "So What"

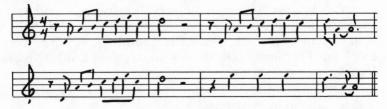

The relative simplicity of the harmonic construction of "So What" is illustrated by the diagram of its structure given as Example 5. The implications for improvisation should be compared with those of the previous practice as exhibited in Examples 1–3.

Miles Davis and a sextet under his leadership are generally credited with making the first practical experiments with the use of modal scales in jazz.[4] "Milestones," from the recording *Milestones* (Columbia CL–1193, 1958), was the first example of employing melodic improvisations based on modal scales in the place of a series of chords. In this piece vertical chordal movement was reduced to a minimum, one chord for each section, by

Example 5. The Harmonic Scheme of "So What"

A	A	B	A
8mm	8mm	8mm	8mm
D Dorian	D Dorian	E-flat Dorian	D Dorian

assigning a Dorian scale built on G for the A sections and an Aeolian scale built on A for the B sections. The formal scheme is AABBA.

The ease with which the Davis sextet made the transition from improvising on chord changes to improvising within the much narrower framework was facilitated by the nature of the melodic patterns chosen. The Aeolian scale is identical to the natural minor scale of traditional harmony. The Dorian scale is similar to a scale built of pitches used in playing the blues, the so-called "blues" scale. This similarity is shown in Example 6. It is likely that this similarity caused the Dorian scale to become the most commonly employed modal resource in jazz.

Example 6. Comparison of Dorian Scale and "Blues" Scale

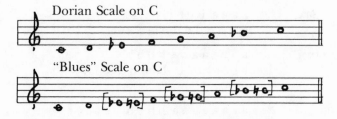

Kind of Blue (Columbia CS–8163, 1959), recorded almost one year later with the same personnel, was a continuation of Davis's exploration of modal improvisation and was the first example of modal playing by saxophonist John Coltrane. Davis and Coltrane became the central figures in the early phase of modal playing.

In addition to establishing the method of employing modal scales found in "So What," which may be seen as a modification and simplification of previous practice, this album contained an example of a different type of treatment, one less structured. The pitch resources of "Flamenco Sketches" are derived from a series of five modal scales: Ionian on C, Ionian on A-flat, Ionian on B-flat, Phrygian on D, and Aeolian on G. There is no theme. In itself this is not novel. The blues, for example, has no theme as such, but it does have a preconceived harmonic structure and a tradition of melodic practices. In "Flamenco Sketches" there is no melody or chord progression for variation. The piece proceeds as a series of solo improvisation in which the only fixed elements are the meter and the order of the five modal scales. Each soloist is responsible for determining the length and structural details of his solo and, more significantly, for how long each modal scale will be used. Example 7, a diagram based on information presented by Jost,[5] illustrates the length of each solo and the subdivisions by scale usage. The changes in letters represent the changes in scalar material; each appearance of a letter represents one measure.

Example 7. The Structural Design of "Flamenco Sketches"

piano	4	a a a a
trumpet	24	a a a a b b b b c c c c d d d d d d d d e e e e
tenor sax	24	a a a a b b b b c c c c d d d d d d d d e e e e
alto sax	33	a a a a a a a a b b b b c c c c c c c c d d d d d d d d e e e e
piano	28	a a a a a a a a b b b b c c c c c c c c d d d d e e e e
trumpet	22	a a a a b b b b c c c c d d d d d d d d e e

This procedure of establishing a small number of fixed elements and leaving the remainder to performer choice was a noteworthy development in the re-evaluation of ensemble playing.

In general, however, the early phase of modal playing was a conservative venture in that the use of modal scales was grafted onto inherited forms and the inherited tonal framework and organized within the limitations of the inherited metric patterns. The possibilities suggested by the dismissal of regulated measure patterns for solos in "Flamenco Sketches" were largely ignored.

In October of 1960, John Coltrane, after having recorded *Giant Steps* (Atlantic 1311, 1960), in which he exhibited an unqualified mastery in executing the older procedure of playing the chord changes, returned to modal playing with the recording *My Favorite Things* (Atlantic 1361, 1960). Coltrane's treatment of modal principles was much freer. In the Davis group soloists relied heavily on the pitches of the designated modal scale and employed foreign tones for ornamental or passing-tone purposes. The periodic divisions of the theme were usually apparent in the phrasing and structure of the solos. In the context of his own ensemble, Coltrane expanded the pitch material by including more pitches outside of the modal scale and by placing these pitches at musically important points for expressive purposes. The prevalence of irregular phrasing tended to obscure the four- and eight-measure divisions of the substructure.

Thus, as early as the end of 1960, the limitations of the modal system were already apparent. Coltrane's example set the stage for further encroachments to the integrity of the modal scale as an organizational feature. In some later pieces, such as "India" from the collection *Impressions* (Impulse AS–42, 1961/63), the ability of the modal scale to act as a unifying agent was severely damaged by the presence of foreign pitches. This fact, accompanied by experiments with nontraditional through-composed forms and the obscurity of the bar line resulted in music "difficult" for listeners in comparison to earlier modal pieces. In others, the respect for the modal material was maintained. "Alabama" from the recording *Live at Birdland* (Impulse AS–50, 1963), for example, is almost transparent in its sectional design and adherence to almost old-fashioned practices.

The use of modal scales remained an important feature of jazz through the sixties, with the procedures established by Davis and Coltrane serving as models for other small groups and big bands as well. Coltrane became a "cult figure" to members of the black avant-garde movement, and his experimental practices became the cornerstone for the development of "free jazz." After 1966, Davis led the way to the use of modal scales in a new setting, rock-inspired jazz, which also became widely imitated.

The whole matter of modal playing did not leave more conservative jazz artists untouched. Those jazz artists who still relied upon harmonic constructions as a basis for improvisation shared with the modal experimenters a common desire to obscure harmony. Although these musicians continued to play the changes, they developed a new vocabulary of chord scales that pushed the harmonic content of their music to new levels of expression and

WILLIAM RANSOM HOGAN
JAZZ ARCHIVE
TULANE UNIVERSITY
NEW ORLEANS

tension. These chord scales included alterations of previously used chord scales, modal patterns, pentatonic scales, and synthetic scales.

For example, in a lecture at the University of Iowa on April 6, 1976, Nicolas Slonimsky reported that his publisher had informed him that Coltrane had recommended Slonimsky's *Thesaurus of Scales and Melodic Patterns* (New York: Coleman-Ross, 1947) to all his colleagues and pupils. This work, which contains nearly 1,000 traditional and contrived scales, is described by its author as a "reference book for composers in search of new materials." Coltrane's use of Slonimsky's *Thesaurus* as a personal practice tool is confirmed in Thomas's account of a private practice session by Coltrane.[6]

A direct relationship between the introduction of modal scales into jazz and an interest in the church modes of the Middle Ages is highly doubtful. Equally improbable is the premise that initial experiments with modal patterns were references to the Indian *rāga* or the melodic orientations of other non-Western musics. The fascination with the music of other cultures to the extent that would arise a few years later had not yet appeared. Jost argues that modal playing

> came about spontaneously at a point in jazz history when the rigidity of the harmonic framework had brought about the perpetual reinterpretation of traditional patterns, no matter how sophisticated they may have become in the meantime.[7]

Although there is truth in this statement, the introduction of modal scales into jazz was undoubtedly influenced by their use in Western fine-art music earlier in the twentieth century. This was not, however, a simple or calculated borrowing. The idiomatic application of these resources to jazz improvisation was the result of the ingenuity of jazz musicians. Berendt, nevertheless, emphasizes the similarity of modal playing with practices common in other cultures and implies a relationship between exotic practice and the appearance of modal scales in jazz.[8]

The Introduction of Non-Western Melodic Resources

By at least 1963 the American jazz musicians' interest in world musics began to manifest itself. Affectations of non-

Western melodic practices began to appear in jazz compositions. Many early efforts were rather uncomplicated quotations of melodies and scales, not necessarily attempts at synthetic combination of styles. The adaptation of Asian and North African melodic materials in the music of Yusef Lateef illustrates this point.

It is a rather safe assumption that by this time the similarity of modal practice in jazz and the melodic orientation of other world musics was recognized by jazz musicians. Indian music and its concept of *rāga* attracted the interest of a substantial number of jazz musicians who sought to refine the melodic organization of their improvisations in the absence of chord progressions. The following statement by Eric Dolphy about Indian music illustrates this concern for learning to deal successfully with a reduced harmonic architecture for improvisation:

> I've talked with Ravi Shankar and I see how we can incorporate their ideas . . . Indian music sounds to us like one minor chord; they call it a Raga or scale and they'll play on one for twenty minutes . . . it's a challenge to play a long time on just one or two chords.[9]

Although this comment does not indicate a great understanding of Indian musical practice on Dolphy's part, it does confirm the close relationship between the use of modal scales in jazz and the investigation of non-Western improvisatory methods by jazz musicians.

The *rāga* is a specialized tonal frame represented in part by a specific pitch grouping derived from the seventy-two parent scales of Indian music. Kaufmann presents the following qualifications in his attempt to define succinctly the difficult term "rāga":

> (1) A *rāga* may be represented by a scale which may or may not possess the same notes in ascent and descent; most *rāgas* differ from each other in their specific tone material. (2) There are some *rāgas* which cannot be represented by simple scale forms because their scales ascend and/or descend in a more or less irregular manner, e.g., in a zigzag. (3) Certain tones within the tone material of a *rāga* have greater, others lesser, importance; in some instances several *rāgas* with identical tone material are distinguished from each other by the different emphasis given to specific notes. (4) Numerous *rāgas* are characterized by certain typical

phrases, other *rāgas* by certain typical intonations of some
of their notes. (5) All *rāgas* are performed to the sound of
characteristic drones.[10]

With an awareness of all essential features of a chosen *rāga* and
with regard for rhythm and structural design, the performer
improvises.

The impact of the *rāga* tradition on jazz, in spite of the
professed interest and admiration of many jazz musicians, was
necessarily limited. During the sixties, jazz artists were primarily
concerned with expanding the range of their musical resources,
not with succumbing to a completely foreign discipline. With
respect to the music of India, this search took the form of borrowing specific elements such as individual *rāga* scales and
melodic patterns, the idea of the drone, and characteristic
rhythmic patterns. This material was incorporated then into a
jazz context.

The efforts of jazz critics to compare jazz performances with
improvisation within a *rāga*, with few exceptions, is completely
naive. For example, Frank Kofsky's attempt to find common
ground between authentic Indian practices and Coltrane's tribute to Indian music, "India" from the recording *Impressions* (Impulse AS–42, 1961/63), is misguided and misleading.[11] That
piece is an example of the use of modal scales with Indian affectations. It is an evocation of Indian music, rather than a synthesis or even an imitation.

There were, however, attempts at fusing the two traditions.
The composition *Synthesis* by Don Ellis, premiered by the Hindustani Jazz Sextet and the Los Angeles Neophonic Orchestra in
1966, displayed the use of two contrasting *rāga* as sources of
melodic material and as a basis for improvisation. Other Indian
references included the presence of Indian instruments and
rhythms. The piece is also distinctive for the development of a
unique hybrid, Indian "scat" singing, in which members of the
sextet imitated the sounds of the *tabla* with nonsense syllables.[12]
Another example of Ellis's use of the *rāga* concept in a jazz style
is his composition "New Nine," found on the album *Live at Monterrey* (Pacific Jazz 20112, 1965). Its melodic material is derived
from a *rāga* and the blues.

The most serious attempt at authenticity in the use of Indian materials during the decade is found on two recordings by flutist Paul Horn with the assistance of native Indian instrumentalists: *Paul Horn in India* (World Pacific WPS–21447, 1967) and *Paul Horn in Kashmir* (World Pacific WPS–1445, 1967). The former album was a cooperative venture between Horn and pupils of Ravi Shankar. Shankar himself selected which *rāgas* the group would use and composed three original melodies based on ancient *rāgas* for the recording.[13] The latter recording features Horn and a group of Kashmiri musicians favored by Horn's spiritual teacher, the Maharishi Yogi, who shared in the planning of its contents and to whom the music is dedicated.[14] On both recordings the individual pieces are identified by the *rāga* used.

These albums do not represent a fusion of jazz and the *rāga* in an overt sense because of Horn's sincere attempt to imitate Indian practice, to improvise within the *rāga* system, and to approximate the sound of the classical bamboo flute of India on its modern European counterpart. The performances are of consequence, nonetheless, because of the example they provided for Horn's colleagues and because traces of Horn's jazz background can be detected in his impassioned solo improvisation.

The Use of Quartal Harmony

During the sixties jazz musicians also made great use of quartal harmony, the construction of both the vertical and horizontal aspects of the music on the interval of the fourth. Like modal scales, quartal harmony is a musical anachronism and was altered to accommodate a key center. Many quartal effects, such as stating thematic material in parallel fourths, building chords of superimposed fourths, and constructing melodic lines by means of consecutive or displaced fourths, were used with such regularity that they soon lost their original expressive character and became accepted as standard procedures for enriching and obscuring tonal jazz. The use of quartal harmony is, perhaps, most evident in the accompaniments and solos of jazz pianists, for example, McCoy Tyner, Bill Evans, and Herbie Hancock. Quartal harmony may be seen as an extension of the chromatic harmony of the jazz of the fifties. A similar development took place earlier in the twentieth century in fine-art music after the culmination of the nineteenth-century romantic style.

The Use of Polytonality

Another technique employed by jazz musicians to ensure harmonic ambiguity was that of deliberately constructing a background that implied more than one tonal center. This was done by placing a triad defining one tonality over a foundation bass pitch that implied another. The soloist then remained free to choose either of the suggested key areas or to establish a third. This practice was an extension of a principle established in the bop style, in which a mild bitonality had been suggested by soloists' emphasis of the seventh, eleventh, and thirteenth degree of a tertial chord.

This kind of harmonic treatment appeared in the more controlled realm of jazz composition for large ensembles as well as in the music of small combos. Herbie Hancock's performance of "Maiden Voyage" from his album *Maiden Voyage* (Blue Note BLP–4195/84195, 1965) is an example of the presence of bitonality in the improvised background to a jazz solo.

THE ABSENCE OF A TONAL CENTER

In the preceding sections several extensions to the system of functional harmony have been described. All of these practices were based on the presence of a tonal center. Concurrent with the development of these methods was an equally important movement in which jazz musicians engaged in the creation of music in which they sought to negate the principle of tonality.

The Use of Serial Procedures

Under the influence of twentieth-century fine-art composers, a number of jazz composers began to consider whether serial procedures could be adapted to their own purposes. The use of dodecaphonic techniques in conjunction with elements of jazz was not without precedent. Several European composers of fine-art music had experimented with integrating the two styles earlier in the century. Ernst Krenek had employed twelve-tone compositional techniques in his jazz-inspired opera of 1927,

Jonny spielt auf. It is reported that Matyas Seiber composed a piece in 1932 entitled "Jazzolette," in which pitch was determined by a row and other features were based on the jazz of the day.[15] Rolf Liebermann's *Concerto for Jazzband and Orchestra* of 1954 exhibits similar procedures in a concerto grosso-like texture. This latter composition served as the prototype for a number of third-stream pieces produced in the sixties.

The introduction of serial procedures into jazz during the sixties was the result of the artistic goals of musicians much more closely related to the jazz tradition, either as performers or composers. The percentage of jazz pieces employing serialism was not large. Their existence, nonetheless, represents another avenue of investigation fostered by the general dissatisfaction with the inherited harmonic practice.

Jazz critic and historian Leonard Feather has credited himself with composing in 1959 the first jazz piece in which serial techniques were applied to the blues:

> The idea came to me in 1959 shortly after a reading of H. H. Stuckenschmidt's book on the principles of the Schoenberg 12-tone system. The self-challenge was (a) to use the form of the blues, yet somehow combine it with the seemingly incompatible essence of the dodecaphonic technique, (b) to make the line swing horizontally, (c) to give it a rhythmic and melodic variety strong enough to avoid rifflike repetitiousness or monotony.[16]

In "Twelve-Tone Blues," Feather applied dodecaphonic procedures to the melody only. The tone row, given as Example 8, is presented in its original form in the first two measures.

Example 8. The Tone Row in "Twelve-Tone Blues"

In the construction of the melody, Feather uses the tone row in its original, retrograde, and retrograde inversion forms. He uses only one transposition, the original a fourth higher to comply with the movement to the subdominant in the blues progression. As a foundation to this rudimentary manipulation of the row, Feather supplies a fairly conventional modern blues bass line.

He indicates the use of chromatically altered ninth chords for the purposes of harmonization and the use of the whole tone scale for the purpose of improvisation. He makes no reference to the possibility of serial improvisation. The piece is printed in *down beat* 33 (February 24, 1966), 17.

Another example of the use of the tone row as a means of melodic construction in a jazz piece can be found in the composition "T.T.T." (Twelve Tone Tune) by pianist Bill Evans, recorded on *The Bill Evans Album* (Columbia C–30855, 1971). The melody of the thematic section consists of three statements of a twelve-tone row with octave displacement changing the contour of the melodic line in each repetition. Its harmonization is unquestionably tonal with its conspicuous reliance upon the circle of fifths and secondary dominants. The use of chromatic alterations, quartal constructions, and other pandiatonic effects create an obscured harmonic language appropriate to the use of the twelve-tone melody.

Evans perceives his application of serialism as a conditional challenge:

> The whole challenge of it is to find a row and use it in such a way that it fits a traditional harmonic form and the sound of jazz, like blues or any logical thing. . . .[17]

This purpose is clearly one of grafting the concept of the tone row onto a tonal foundation. The advanced state of Evans's harmonic vocabulary makes his introduction of the chromatic melody seem not incongruous. The tone row of the piece and the harmonization of the thematic section are presented in Example 9.

In addition to its use for purely melodic purposes, serialism became part of the technical language for constructing atonal backgrounds for "free" improvisation and for organizing large ensemble jazz. A host of jazz composers and arrangers, most of them associated with the artistic goals of the Third Stream Movement, employed the tone row as the organizing agent-for ensemble sections and for ensemble accompaniments to solos. Several works of Gunther Schuller are representative of these methods. "Conversation," a dialogue between serially composed music for a string quartet and collectively improvised music of the Modern Jazz Quartet, is found on the recording *Third Stream*

Example 9. "T.T.T.": The Tone Row and the Thematic Section[18]

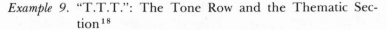

Music (Atlantic 1345, 1960). *Abstraction*, from the recording *Jazz Abstractions* by various artists (Atlantic 1365, 1961), is an example of a serially composed background onto which saxophonist Ornette Coleman superimposed an improvised "atonal" solo. Of this venture, Schuller has written:

> It seems to me that there are many parallels between the playing of Ornette Coleman and so-called serial music, parallels which *Abstraction* tries to isolate and underscore. Not only is Ornette's choice of notes sufficiently freed to function against an atonal, serialized background, but the type of non-thematic continuity he projects — outwardly fragmentary, but inwardly cohesive — is very similar to that of recent developments in contemporary non-jazz music.[19]

57

At least one example within this category of jazz composition, *The Ritual of Sound* (ca. 1963) by Lalo Schifrin, exhibited the serial organization of other parameters of the piece in addition to pitch. The following description appeared in the program notes written by the composer for a 1963 performance:

> The thirteen-piece instrumental ensemble is used so as to achieve textures which are determined by serially derived degrees of density and timbral associations, both singly and in combination. In order to locate this sound material in sound space, registral displacement was determined on the basis of a numerical series derived from the original pitch series.[20]

The ultimate validity of the application of serial techniques to jazz rests with the capability to improvise according to its precepts. In 1964 composer John Benson Brooks announced that he had worked out a system for improvising with the tone row.[21] Brooks imposed the following conditions on his system: (1) rhythm should be free of metric restrictions; (2) the use of the row in improvisation should be analogous to traditional methods; (3) octave displacement of row pitches is acceptable; and (4) the basic shape of the row (the order of pitches) should be retained in order that the formal aspects of serial procedures are not lost.[22]

These prescriptions, however, have little bearing on the inherent obstacle of serial improvisation, the memorization of the row in its various forms and transpositions. Brooks's permission for the improviser to "jump from any note in the row to any other, so long as he then continues the forward motion of the row" or to engage in "conditional repetition," the repetition of row motives,[23] would appear to be causes for confusion rather than assistance.

In spite of the efforts by Brooks and some others, most notably pianist Walter Bishop, Jr., and critic and alto saxophonist Don Heckman, improvisation based on twelve-tone principles did not become a viable part of the jazz soloist's art. Difficulties aside, jazz musicians who had "escaped" from the yoke of functional harmony were, perhaps, simply unwilling to replace it with a method more exacting and, in many ways, more structured.

The Use of Other Atonal Procedures

In many other cases, situations in which serial procedures were not in force, there were definite attempts to negate the presence of a tonal center. This was accomplished by completely rejecting the traditional performance framework. The practice of rendering a jazz performance by treating a pre-existing composition was abandoned. The role of functional harmony was also abandoned. This method was replaced by free group improvisation, the simultaneous creation of melodic lines with little or no concern for the production of "harmonious" vertical composites. Often the individual lines are not harmonically complex and clearly reflect a tonal center. For this reason "pantonality" is, perhaps, a more appropriate term than "atonality."

This type of jazz was produced primarily by young black jazz musicians whose music was surrounded by social purpose. At the time Archie Shepp, activist and saxophonist, characterized this music as an attempt to recapture the preharmony practice of "black music" before slavery.[24] Of the relationship between the avant-garde black jazz of the sixties and the "back-to-Africa" aesthetic, Clifford Thornton made the following comments in 1975:

> During the '60s the prevailing opinion seemed to be that free playing *was* a return to African roots, a rejection of Western criteria. But while we were busy feeling that we were returning to the roots, it would have been better put to say that we were *looking* for those roots. In fact, we're just now learning what African music sounds like and how to perform it. It seems so much hysteria was whipped up by the events of the '60s, that our notions of what really constitutes this sense of tradition, of a lineage continuing in our culture, got somewhat out of focus.[25]

This assessment is unquestionably true.

In this type of jazz, it became common practice to eliminate the piano from the instrumentation of the combo. Because of its idiomatic capability for providing chords and, perhaps, because of its traditional role as the provider of the now-discarded chord changes, the presence of the piano tended to inhibit the soloists in their attempt to create melodies free of traditional harmonic considerations. The presence of the piano also tended to upset the balance of equal voices sought in collective improvisation.

Another characteristic of the piano considered detrimental was its equal temperament. Because of the de-emphasis of the tonal center and consequently the relationship of all pitches to it, the necessity of a standard intonation no longer was felt to exist. This development was accompanied by the exploration of vocalized sound and new expressive devices. Alto saxophonist Ornette Coleman, a pioneer in discarding the pre-existing composition and its implications for improvisation, attached an emotional dimension to pitch: "If I play an F in a tune called 'Peace,' I don't think it should sound the same as an F that is supposed to express sadness."[26]

When the piano was retained, it was most often used to provide tone clusters that constantly denied the primacy of any single pitch. In the music of pianist Cecil Taylor, the tone cluster became a stylistic feature. They frequently appear as a series of short, accented sound units executed in rapid succession and covering the entire range of the keyboard.

---

1 See Jerry Coker, *Improvising Jazz* (Englewood Cliffs, N.J.: Prentice-Hall, 1964); John Mehegan, *Jazz Improvisation*, 4 vols. (New York: Watson-Guptill, 1959–65); George Russell, *The Lydian Chromatic Concept of Tonal Organization*, 3d ed. (New York: Concept, 1959).

2 Leon Dallin, *Techniques of Twentieth Century Composition*, 3d ed. (Dubuque, Iowa: Wm. C. Brown, 1974), p. 19.

3 Nat Hentoff, *The Jazz Life* (New York: Dial, 1961), p. 208.

4 In 1953 George Russell published *The Lydian Chromatic Concept of Tonal Organization* (New York: Concept, 1953), an investigation into the potential uses of the Lydian scale for jazz improvisation. The work is both theoretical and practical in nature.

5 Ekkehard Jost, *Free Jazz* (Graz: Universal, 1974), p. 22.

6 J. C. Thomas, *Chasin' the Trane: The Music and Mystique of John Coltrane* (New York: Doubleday, 1975), p. 102.

7 Jost, *Free Jazz*, p. 19.

8 Joachim-Ernst Berendt, *The Jazz Book*, trans. by Dan Morgenstern, Helmut Bredigkeit, and Barbara Bredigkeit (New York: Lawrence Hill, 1975), pp. 155–56.

9 Quoted without documentation in Vladimir Simosko and Barry Tepperman, *Eric Dolphy: A Musical Biography and Discography* (Washington, D.C.: Smithsonian Institution Press, 1974), p. 13.

10 Walter Kaufmann, *The Ragas of North India* (Bloomington, Ind.: Indiana University Press, 1968), p. v.

11 Frank Kofsky, *Black Nationalism and the Revolution in Music* (New York: Pathfinder, 1970), p. 193.

12   Harvey Siders, "Caught in the Act: Los Angeles Neophonic Orchestra," *down beat* 33 (March 24, 1966), 47.

13   Robert Palmer, record liner notes to *Paul Horn in India* by Paul Horn (Blue Note LA529–H2, reissued 1975).

14   *Ibid.*

15   Don Banks, "Converging Streams," *Musical Times* 111 (June 1970), 597.

16   Leonard Feather, "Twelve Tone Blues," *down beat* 33 (February 24, 1966), 17. (Reprinted with permission of *down beat*.) Apparently Feather is referring to H. H. Stuckenschmidt, *Arnold Schönberg*, trans. by Edith Temple Roberts and Humphrey Searle (London: J. Calder, 1959).

17   Fred Binkley, record liner notes to *The Bill Evans Album* by Bill Evans (Columbia C–30855, 1971).

18   Robert L. Brown, "Classical Influences on Jazz." Published by permission of Transaction, Inc. from JOURNAL OF JAZZ STUDIES, Vol 3 #2, Copyright © 1976 by Transaction, Inc.

19   Gunther Schuller, record liner notes to *Jazz Abstractions* by various artists (Atlantic 1365, 1961).

20   Whitney Balliett, *Such Sweet Thunder: Forty-nine Pieces on Jazz* (Indianapolis: Bobbs-Merrill, 1966), pp. 63–64. Reprinted by permission of Harold Ober Associates Incorporated. Copyright © 1966 by Whitney Balliett.

21   Don Heckman, "Sounds and Silence: 12-Tone Music," *down beat* 33 (June 30, 1966), 27.

22   *Ibid.*

23   *Ibid.*

24   LeRoi Jones, "Voice from the Avant Garde: Archie Shepp," *down beat* 32 (January 14, 1965), 20.

25   Robert Palmer, "Clifford Thornton: Flowers in the Garden of Harlem," *down beat* 42 (June 19, 1975), 19. (Reprinted with permission of *down beat*.)

26   Berendt, *The Jazz Book,* p. 110.

Meter and Rhythm

For approximately the first fifty years in the history of jazz, the metric system accepted by jazz musicians to give their music organization in time was straight-forward duple meter: time units with two or four beats. It is as if this relatively simple metric framework was a necessary condition for the music and the musicians to mature in other ways. Within the limitations of duple meter, however, jazz musicians developed an extraordinary sense of timing and a wealth of rhythmic nuances. By the end of the fifties many jazz musicians became convinced that jazz need not be restricted to this metric structure. The process of metric re-evaluation resulted in the production of jazz organized in time in ways unlike any to be found in earlier jazz, as well as jazz organized according to new rhythmic patterns within the older system.

The treatment of meter and rhythm in the jazz of the sixties can be divided into two practices: the presence of a regular pulse and the absence of a regular pulse.

The Presence of a Regular Pulse

Interest in Irregular Meters

New liberties were taken with meter in the mid-fifties. The first departure from the metric norm was the jazz waltz, jazz in 3/4 time. It was soon discovered that jazz could be organized successfully within the new framework without invalidating the concept of swing, which was then held to be an intrinsic feature to any jazz style.

Soon after the general acceptance of the jazz waltz, other experiments with jazz in irregular meter began to occur. The leader of this trend was Dave Brubeck and his quartet. Representative of his music are "Take Five," a piece in 5/4 meter, and "Blue Rondo alla Turk," an exploration of some possibilities of

9/8 meter. He continued this interest throughout the sixties. Sample recordings are *Time Out* (Columbia CS–8192, 1960), *Time Further Out* (Columbia CS–8490, 1961), and *Time Changes* (Columbia CS–2127, 1964).

During the sixties, studies in irregular meter became assimilated into the big-band concept and were particularly championed by Don Ellis and his band, an organization conceived as a workshop experiment in 1964. Examination of several of his recordings from the middle years of the decade exhibits his interest in playing large-ensemble jazz in unconventional, complicated metric situations. The recording *Live in 3⅔/4 Time* (Pacific Jazz PJ–10123, 1967) provides the following examples: "Barnum's Revenge" in 7/4 (subdivided 3–2–2), "Upstart" in 3⅔/4 (11/8), and "Orientation" in 16/8 (subdivided 3–2–2, 3–2–2–2). The recording *Electric Bath* (Columbia CS–9585, 1968) also provides examples: "Open Beauty" in 3½/4, "New Horizons" based on a cycle of 17 (subdivided 5–5–7), and "Indian Lady" in 5/4 (subdivided 3–2). Another celebrated Ellis composition "332221222" from his album *Live at Monterrey* (Pacific Jazz 20112, 1966) is written in what Ellis has called "the traditional 19." The title of the work indicates the subdivision pattern of the 19/4 meter. It has been reported by Jon Balleras that Ellis once wrote a jazz composition cast in a meter of 172/8 [*sic*].[1]

These pieces all exemplify the presence of recurring stress patterns, however intricate. Ellis, moreover, has also shown interest in the principle of variable meter, situations in which the subdivisions of the unit measure are not identical in succession. In the Ellis piece "New Nine" from the *Live at Monterrey* album, the subdivisions of the unit measure are derived from permutations of the binary and ternary groupings of the nine component beats of each measure: 2–2–2–3, 2–2–3–2, 2–3–2–2, 3–2–2–2, 3–3–3.

No matter how unorthodox a time signature may appear, each may be reduced to usually a short series of binary and ternary groupings (as indicated in the preceding paragraphs) and thus may be represented as a composite of two or more simple time signatures. For example, a measure in 5/4 may be constructed of a measure in 3/4 meter followed by one in 2/4, or a measure in 7/4 may be constructed of a measure in 4/4 meter followed by one in 3/4. The foreground rhythmic details accommodate this metric foundation. Examples 10 and 11 illustrate the relationship of the rhythmic construction of the melody and the underlying organization of binary and ternary metric units in the thematic sections of two well-known pieces. In compositions employing irregular meters, the harmonic rhythm typically reinforces the metric scheme. This is also shown in Examples 10 and 11. The coincidence of metric subdivisions and the harmonic rhythm is undoubtedly a convenience for the soloist during improvisation.

Example 10. Relationship of Melodic Rhythm, Meter, and Harmonic Rhythm in "Take Five" by Paul Desmond (*Time Out* by Dave Brubeck, Columbia CS–9192, 1960)

Example 11. Relationship of Melodic Rhythm, Meter, and Harmonic Rhythm in "Pussy Wiggle Stomp" by Don Ellis (*At Fillmore* by Don Ellis, Columbia CG–30243, 1970)

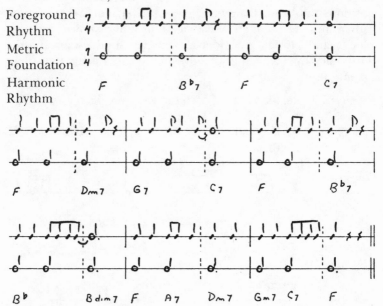

Important conditions for Ellis's explorations of irregular meters have been the primacy of improvisation and the maintenance of the concept of swing. In a 1961 interview, Ellis emphasized these aspects:

> I don't know where jazz is heading but I'd like to see it keep improvisation and swing. And it doesn't have to be sanctified to swing . . . it doesn't always have to be 4/4. There are a lot of other time signatures to try out.[2]

By 1966 Ellis and the members of his ensemble had developed a remarkable metric versatility in their performance of big-band jazz. Leonard Feather has characterized an Ellis performance as

> a kaleidoscope of metric novelties that could swing the tempo [*sic*] of his big band, in the course of a single set, from 5/4 to 5/8 to 13/4 to 27/16 to 6/8, with only a now-and-then glimpse back at that quaint old 4/4 beat that used to be the basis of all jazz.[3]

Ellis has published a codification of his own rhythmic practices and his methods for acquiring the requisite skills for executing them and ultimately improvising according to them. *The New Rhythm Book* (North Hollywood: Ellis Music Enterprises, 1972) is a study of irregular metric patterns derived primarily from the musical traditions of a number of non-American cultures. Close attention is given to the rhythmic practices found in the music of India and in the folk music of Eastern Europe.

It is Ellis's contention that the fine-art music tradition of Europe and the United States is outside of the mainstream with respect to the rhythmic vitality of the music of the rest of the world. Because rhythmic and metrical details considered foreign or difficult by musicians trained in the European tradition are accepted as "natural to a great portion of the world's peoples,"[4] Ellis has encouraged their incorporation into the jazz idiom.

Interest in "new" metrical systems and rhythmic subdivisions was undoubtedly hastened by the exposure of jazz musicians to the music of other cultures. The innovations of Ellis were strongly influenced by the music of India. Rhythm in Indian music is organized according to the additive principle of *tala*, in which successive metrical units may differ from one another and may be given different musical significance. A pattern constructed of several units is then repeated for the duration of the piece. For example, one such *tala* pattern, known as *Rupak*, is comprised of seven beats distributed within three units. This pattern[5] is given in Example 12.

Example 12. The *Tala* Pattern of *Rupak*

Ellis has borrowed this idea of unequal stress and infused it into the Western concept of the measure.

European fine-art music experienced a period of metric and rhythmic re-evaluation after 1910 under the leadership of Bartok, Stravinsky, and Schoenberg. The metrical features of European folk music were introduced into fine-art compositions as one aspect of that development. Complex meter and variable meter became general stylistic traits of twentieth-century fine-art music. This was surely another major influence on the metric experimentation found in the jazz of the sixties.

The Use of Rhythmic Ostinatos

Another important aspect of rhythmic practice in the sixties was the use of rhythmic ostinatos as organizational units. Because earlier jazz had been closely related to popular dancing, the use of characteristic dance rhythms was not at all unfamiliar to jazz musicians. Their application in jazz pieces had been not so much one of literal repetition, but rather that of serving as theme for rhythmic variation. This approach was also adopted in the assimilation of *bossa nova* and rock rhythmic patterns into jazz. Both types of rhythmic formulas were cast in duple meter. Their use represented the continuation of the traditional treatment of meter and rhythm in jazz although the property of swing was less important in both innovations. The *bossa nova* and rock are discussed in Chapter 7.

THE ABSENCE OF A REGULAR PULSE

Experimentation with irregular meters and the adaption of rhythmic ostinatos reflected the tendency of a majority of jazz musicians to continue to organize their music according to the presence of a fixed pulse and a fundamental meter and to exploit the wide range of rhythmic variety inherent in that system. In contrast to this were musicians associated with more "progressive" forces whose rhythmic and metric principles became antithetical to this convention. The necessity of constant pulse, meter, and rhythmic details that periodically affirmed pulse and meter came under serious scrutiny.

There is a noticeable evolution in the development of these principles. Their foundation was, of course, the stricter rhythmic and metric practices of earlier jazz. Periodically in the combo jazz of the late fifties and early sixties, the musicians break through the time structure — depart from it and obscure it — and then return to it. A relatively simple example of this is the establishment of triple metric patterns in an otherwise duple framework. This was an expressive device, a means of creating rhythmic tension to be resolved only by a confirmation of the original stress pattern. This device was used in much the same way and for the same reason, and often at the same time, that musicians departed from the established harmonic structure, created harmonic tension with dissonance, only to be relieved by a return to the previously established tonal center. This technique can be heard on recordings of the music of ensembles led by Miles Davis and John Coltrane in the late fifties and early sixties. The drumming of Elvin Jones is particularly illustrative of obscuring meter.

The example of Ornette Coleman was extremely important in the development of the new attitude toward rhythm and meter. Coleman achieved immediate notoriety in November of 1959 for his innovative approach to jazz-making. He summarized his concept of time in the following manner:

> . . . my music doesn't have any real time, no metric time. It has time, but not in the sense that you can time it. It's more like breathing, a natural, freer time. . . . I like spread rhythm, rhythm that has a lot of freedom in it, rather than the more conventional, *netted* rhythm. With spread rhythm, you might tap your feet awhile, then stop, then later start tapping again. That's what I like. Otherwise, you tap your feet so much, you forget what you hear. You just hear the rhythm.[6]

This type of *tempo rubato,* once employed in jazz for dramatic effects in introductory, transitional, or coda sections, became a standard procedure for negating the metronomic strictness of the earlier practice. *The Shape of Jazz to Come* (Atlantic 1317, 1959) and *Change of the Century* (Atlantic 1327, 1959) by Coleman contain examples.

A more systematic, but equally novel attack on the constant pulse of jazz emerged in the use of tempo changes. Tempo distortion by means of *accelerando* and *decelerando* added a new dimension to jazz performance practice. Jost reports that in the music of Charles Mingus the initial tempo is rarely maintained throughout a composition and that accelerations of up to four times the original tempo are not at all unusual.[7] Examples of this type of tempo manipulation can be found on *How Time Passes* by Don Ellis (Candid 8004, 1961) and *The Black Saint and the Sinner Lady* by Charles Mingus (Impulse AS–35, 1963).

This concern for obscuring meter, for creating abstract time composites, became quite important in the realm of collective improvisation. It was achieved by what might be called "the diffusion of rhythm." The duties of the rhythm section were preempted. Rhythmic energy became a characteristic of each voice in the texture. Stereotyped rhythmic formulas, especially metric units suggesting stress patterns, were usually avoided. The concept of the bar line, if applicable at all, existed only in theory. The density of the texture was a contributing factor to the creation of metric ambiguity in itself. The absence of temporal reference points posed new problems for the improviser, but the disorientation undoubtedly experienced by the participating musicians as well as the listener was the desired effect. Representative recordings of this practice include *Free Jazz* by Ornette Coleman (Atlantic 1364, 1960), *Ascension* by John Coltrane (Impulse AS–95, 1965), and *Unit Structures* by Cecil Taylor (Blue Note 84237, 1966).

This radical approach to meter and rhythm in effect destroyed the foundation that was conditional for the existence of the property of swing. The absence of swing, a characteristic in some form of all previous jazz styles, is symbolic of the drastic changes in attitude experienced by many jazz musicians, most notably those associated with the black avant-garde in the early sixties.

---

1 Jon Balleras, a review of *The New Rhythm Book* by Don Ellis (North Hollywood: Ellis Music Enterprises, 1972), in *down beat* 40 (November 22, 1973), 34.
2 Leonard Feather, *From Satchmo to Miles* (New York: Stein & Day, 1972), p. 217.
3 *Ibid.*
4 Balleras, review of *New Rhythm Book*, 34.
5 Walter Kaufmann, "India," *Harvard Dictionary of Music*, 2d ed., ed. by Willi Apel (Cambridge, Mass.: Belknap, 1969), p. 409.
6 Joe Goldberg, *Jazz Masters of the Fifties* (New York: Macmillan, 1965), p. 239.
7 Ekkehard Jost, *Free Jazz* (Graz: Universal, 1974), p. 40.

Structural Design

The one requisite consideration for the musical structure of jazz compositions is the accommodation of the improviser. Historically this requirement was satisfied by the use of the theme and variations employed in the manner of a chaconne, the chord structure remaining fixed throughout the set of variations. The exceptions to this design, those devised by the jazz composer-arranger, were reactions to the symmetry and relative simplicity of this formal convention. Deviations often included the manufacturing of introductions and transitional passages and the transposition of sections of theme to related key areas.

Dissatisfaction with this convention led jazz musicians to seek different solutions to the matter of structural design. In the fifties a preoccupation with the structure of jazz pieces in certain circles resulted in a review of European art-music procedures and in experiments with rondo and fugal devices. By the end of that decade, structural experimentation in jazz manifested itself in the appearance of two rather contradictory trends: carefully determining musical structure prior to performance, an emphasis on composition, and allowing musical structure to "happen" during performance in accordance with a small number of fixed elements, an emphasis on improvisation. Both attitudes remained in effect throughout the sixties. Jazz produced according to the prescription of each method existed alongside jazz cast in the older theme-and-variations format.

THIRD STREAM MUSIC

Intentions and Procedures

In a lecture on August 17, 1957, at the Berkshire Music Center in Tanglewood, Massachusetts, Gunther Schuller used the phrase "third-stream" to describe a kind of music that had appeared in which elements of the jazz tradition and of the

71

European fine-art music tradition were intentionally combined. With his documentation of the first appearance of the term, Slonimsky provides the following definition:

> If the first stream is classical and the second stream is jazz, Third Stream is their Hegelian synthesis, which unites and reconciles the classical thesis with the popular antithesis.[1]

The widespread recognition that such a movement was in progress brought forth a barrage of sensational criticism from purists on both sides of the issue. Schuller, who became the most eloquent spokesman for the third-stream ideal by means of lectures and essays as well as his own music, defended his cause and described its origins:

> I coined the term as an *adjective,* not a noun. I never thought it would become a slogan, a catchword. I hit upon the term simply as a handle, and it has achieved a kind of pompousness and finality that are totally inaccurate. I conceive of it as the result of two tributaries — one from the stream of classical music and one from the other stream, jazz — that have recently flowed out toward each other in the space between the two main streams. The two main streams are left undisturbed, or mostly so. I'm often criticized for trying to *force* classical music and jazz together. But this is nonsense. There will always be jazz musicians who have absolutely no knowledge of classical music, and classical musicians and composers who abhor jazz. But if a person has been exposed to both streams honestly and thoroughly, it's bound to show up in his creative products, and those of us who see this possible alignment have the great privilege of working toward it.[2]

It is likely that the artistic objectives of third stream music were logical outgrowths of the "advancement" of the jazz of the fifties. Whereas in previous times, jazz and European fine-art music had been distant in technical regards, actual musical language, and emotional content, the gap between the two musics had been considerably diminished. Enough common ground existed at this time for a composition and performance method that could encompass both traditions on some sort of equal basis.

Possibly of more significance to the development of the third stream was the emergence of a new "breed" of musician, artists like Schuller himself who could perform authoritatively in both idioms. It was the appearance of musicians who could bring together improvisational skills and the sense of timing found in jazz performance and the disciplined requirements of fine-art music that differentiated the third-stream movement from earlier attempts to fuse the two idioms. The initial discovery of jazz by European and American fine-art composers in the twenties resulted in superficial borrowings from jazz in an otherwise European context. Such projects, if in fact they were intended to be more than an exploitation of an exotic "folk music," were conditioned by the limited knowledge and understanding of jazz on the part of composers and by the absence of performers who could meet the demands of playing in both styles. The role of improvisation in such ventures was nonexistent.

A major concern of the third stream was to deliver jazz in the shape of European forms and to employ European compositional techniques. This desire to use formal schemes and integrative devices borrowed from Western fine-art music effected the replacement of the theme-and-variations format with the canon, the fugue, the rondo, the passacaglia, and even sonata principles. Multi-movement forms such as the suite, the sonata cycle, the cantata, and movement couplings (prelude and fugue, passacaglia and fugue) also appeared. Imitative counterpoint, motivic development, and serial devices received much emphasis.

Because of this emphasis placed on the composed element of third stream music, many of the early experiments lacked the quality of spontaneity and the rhythmic flexibility that was so much a part of the jazz tradition. The harnessing of improvisation and its subordination to more complicated structural patterns were results of a compromise between the two ingredients.

Third Stream Music (Atlantic 1345, 1960), a recording of compositions by Schuller, John Lewis, and Jimmy Giuffre performed by the Modern Jazz Quartet, the Beaux Arts String Quartet, and the Jimmy Giuffre Three, provides early examples of the attempt to fuse the two musics. Two of the pieces, "Sketch" by Lewis and "Conversation" by Schuller, combine the forces of the Modern Jazz Quartet (piano, vibraharp, string bass, and drums) and the string quartet and exhibit the alternation of composed and improvised sections. The two pieces performed by the Modern Jazz Quartet and the Jimmy Giuffre Three (clarinet or tenor saxophone, guitar, and string bass) are more evidently studies of classical techniques. "Da Capo" by Lewis is based on the alternating development of two contrasting melodic ideas, the first animated and the second lyrical. "Fine" by Giuffre is cast in rondo form. The difficulty encountered in distinguishing written lines from improvised lines in the latter piece sets it apart from the other selections on the recording.

The most conspicuous structural approach employed on *Third Stream Music* and in much other music created according to its tenets is the alternation of idioms: the alternation of composed sections and improvised sections. Two categories of third-stream compositions also appeared: those exhibiting European techniques within the context of a jazz performing medium and those combining a jazz ensemble with ensembles established by European practice. Uniting the symphony orchestra and a jazz ensemble in concerto grosso fashion became a favored procedure. In such compositions the juxtaposition of contrasting blocks of sound coincided with the alternation of composed and improvised sections. *Variants for Jazz Quartet and Orchestra* (1960) by Gunther Schuller, *Dialogues for Jazz Combo and Symphony Orchestra* (1960) by Howard Brubeck, *Improvisations for Orchestra and Jazz Soloists* (1961) by Larry Austin, and *Three Pieces for Blues Band and Orchestra* (1968) by William Russo are representative of this latter category.

The Leadership of the Modern Jazz Quartet

The Modern Jazz Quartet, one of the longest enduring ensembles in the history of jazz, played a prominent leadership role in the development of third stream music. The group, which was active from 1952 to 1974, was comprised of John Lewis, piano; Milt Jackson, vibraharp; Percy Heath, bass; and Connie Kay, drums. Its original drummer, Kenny Clarke, was replaced by Kay in 1955. The longevity of this partnership and the opportunity to perform regularly and frequently resulted in a high level of musical cooperation and in the refinement of experimental procedures.

Pianist John Lewis was primarily responsible for the musical direction of the quartet as the composer and arranger of much of its repertory. In the fifties he became interested in incorporating the devices, forms, and techniques of European fine-art music into jazz composition. The self-consciousness of these methods to the performers and listeners alike at that time have, through years of familiarity, become functional and natural. A comparison of early recordings with *European Concert* (Atlantic 2–603) of 1960, on which a majority of the pieces had been previously recorded, reveals the superiority of later versions. Of this recording commentator Goldberg has written:

> The MJQ has long been known as one of the few jazz groups which truly improvises, and never allows routines to become set. But the recording is a testament to more than that. It is a testament to the work of Lewis in training the other members in methods originally uncomfortable to them, and in finally making those methods the basic, understood vocabulary of the group, so that the powerful jazz sense of the individual players could function out of that vocabulary.[3]

Lewis has long been known for his fascination for string instruments. In close association with Gunther Schuller, he sought a method for including the symphony orchestra in the performance of jazz. He hoped to accomplish this by supervising the creation of a repertoire of original works for the Modern Jazz Quartet to perform with orchestra. Composers William O. Smith, J. J. Johnson, André Hodeir, Schuller, and Lewis himself accepted commissions for such works. In 1961 the quartet appeared with an orchestra, the Cincinnati Symphony, for the first time. By the time of its dissolution in 1974, the Modern Jazz Quartet had performed with thirty-three major symphony orchestras in the United States and Europe and had premiered a sizable number of third-stream works.

The example of the Modern Jazz Quartet served as a model for the performance of a number of new compositions scored for jazz ensemble and orchestra throughout the decade. Other jazz ensembles, most notably those led by Dave Brubeck, Don Ellis, and Chuck Mangione, took part in similar musical experiences. Lewis and Schuller even organized and directed a short-lived orchestra, known as Orchestra U.S.A., which came into existence for the purpose of performing third-stream compositions. The twenty-nine-piece group was comprised of approximately an equal number of jazz musicians and "legitimate" musicians. The group was active around 1963. Guest soloists with Orchestra U.S.A. included such prominent jazz artists as Ornette Coleman, Gerry Mulligan, Eric Dolphy, and, of course, Lewis himself.

Stan Kenton's Neophonic Orchestra

The re-emergence of Stan Kenton and his founding of the Los Angeles Neophonic Orchestra in 1965 were also manifestations of the third-stream movement. This band of studio musicians, initially without strings, was established by Kenton to provide a performance forum for new music written for large jazz ensembles in the big-band tradition. The format, however, was not much different from Kenton's activities of the previous decade. The term "neophonic" was coined as a distinguishing adjective analogous to "philharmonic." [4]

Although Kenton dismissed any pretension to third-stream idealism,[5] the music performed by the Neophonic Orchestra did reflect many of the innovations championed by Lewis and Schuller. The repertory of the group included such works as *Music for Piano and Band,* No. 2, by Friedrich Gulda, a concerto for jazz pianist and big band; *Prelude and Fugue* by John Williams; *Passacaglia and Fugue* by Allyn Ferguson; and *Adventures in Emotion* by Russ Garcia, a suite of character pieces. The Neophonic Orchestra survived only two seasons of concerts before disbanding. The recording *Stan Kenton Conducts the Los Angeles Neophonic Orchestra* (Capitol MAS–2424, 1965) is a musical souvenir of this enterprise.

Other Applications of Third-Stream Techniques

There is also evidence that other jazz figures were seeking to add substance to their music by adopting European formal elements, but, like Kenton, did not choose to associate themselves with the third-stream movement or to acknowledge their preoccupation with structural design. Because these artists sought to incorporate the new without sacrificing any aspect of the older practice, their methods exhibited greater subtlety.

Representative of this group was Oliver Nelson, jazz composer and saxophonist. An example of his ability to integrate European features into a big-band setting is found in "Sound

Piece for Jazz Orchestra" (1964–65) from his recording *Sound Pieces* (Impulse S–9129, 1967). In this composition a single melodic motive serves as the basis for contrasting thematic ideas, accompanimental patterns, and Nelson's own improvisations on soprano saxophone. The scheme of the work suggests the sonata cycle: a fast, academic first movement with motivic development; a slow, lyrical second movement in song form; and a light-weight finale. The movements are separated by a short pause. The presence of theme transformation, of a cyclic treatment of theme, and of joining movements into one continuous piece suggests a similarity to nineteenth-century European approaches to the sonata cycle. On the other hand, the work is presented in jazz style and makes prominent use of improvisation, the blues, and the riff.

Another manifestation of this type of jazz composition was the popularity of the "jazz suite." Such pieces frequently represented a genre of mild program music, often a glorification or depiction of aspects of Afro-American life, and were designed in the form of a multi-movement composition with each component a character piece, its topic indicated by its title. The performing medium was typically a large jazz ensemble, although not always. Examples of the multi-movement program suite from the sixties are:

Maiden Voyage by Herbie Hancock, performed by a quintet led by Hancock (Blue Note BLP–4195, 1965); a depiction of the sea[6]

> Maiden Voyage
> The Eye of the Hurricane
> Little One
> Survival of the Fittest
> Dolphin Dance

Afro-American Sketches by Oliver Nelson, for big band (Prestige S–7225, 1969); a musical treatment of Afro-American history

> Message
> Jungleaire
> Emancipation Blues

There's a Yearnin'
Going Up North
Disillusioned
Freedom Dance

New Orleans Suite by Duke Ellington, for big band (Atlantic SD–1580, 1971); a musical remembrance of the role of New Orleans in the history of jazz, commissioned by George Wein for the 1970 New Orleans Jazz Festival

Blues for New Orleans
Bourbon Street Jingling Jollies
Portrait of Louis Armstrong
Thanks for the Beautiful Land on the Delta
Portrait of Wellman Braud
Second Line (the funereal band)
Portrait of Sydney Bechet
Aristocracy à la Jean Lafitte
Portrait of Mahalia Jackson

In fact, Duke Ellington had exhibited an interest in these so-called "extended forms" for several decades and continued to champion such methods until his death. By 1960 his works already included "concerto-substitutes" for various members of his band, multi-movement and multi-section "tone poems," and suites. After that year, he continued to make significant contributions to each genre. He thus provided an important example for other jazz composers such as Charles Mingus and Oliver Nelson.

During the sixties Ellington produced two particularly noteworthy works along these lines: two large-scale, musically-unified works based on religious themes. His First Sacred Concert was presented on September 16, 1965, at Grace Cathedral, San Francisco. Excerpts from this composition are recorded on *A Concert of Sacred Music* (RCA Victor LSP–3582, 1966). His Second Sacred Concert (*Second Sacred Concert,* Prestige P–24045, n.d.) was given its premiere at the Cathedral Church of St. John the Divine in New York City on January 19, 1968.

These "concerts" were substantial multi-movement cantata-like works employing a large number of vocalists and instrumentalists, dancers, and theatrical effects. Ellington's own big band, of course, served as the nucleus. The theme of the first concert was the first four words of the King James Version of the *Bible:* "In the beginning God." The six syllables of this text were assigned to a phrase of six pitches. This motive in various settings and transformations serves as an integrative feature of the entire composition. The First Sacred Concert was scored for Ellington's orchestra, two choirs, and soloists with Ellington as pianist playing a prominent role in the composition.

The Second Sacred Concert, with its general theme "Praise God," was an extension of the first. For this work Ellington added an electric piano for his own use and several children's choirs to offer contrast to the large mass of adult voices. A great variety of musical resources, composition types, and devotional moods characterizes the piece. Its finale, "Praise God and Dance," based on the 150th Psalm, is a recapitulation of the opening music, heightened by a faster tempo and by the appearance of two sets of costumed dancers. The first group

> moved with gestures symbolic of worship in the idiom of modern dance. The second, issuing from behind the band, was swinging all the way with steps and rhythms right out of the Savoy ballroom.[7]

Both of these works illustrate Ellington's use of theatrical and philosophical elements in conjunction with a musical style quite conservative by the standards of the sixties and yet reflect his innovative spirit and his genius for jazz composition.

Similar in intent and method to these Ellington pieces is a "jazz mass" composed by Lalo Schifrin for flutist Paul Horn. This piece was scored for a jazz combo led by Horn, an eight-member chorus, and a twelve-piece chamber orchestra. Excerpts from this work are available on the recording *Jazz Suite on the Mass Text* by Paul Horn (RCA Victor LPM–3414, 1965).

Toward "Freer" Form

The other major trend in the treatment of structural design was approximately the antithesis of employing definite formal schemes and other third-stream principles. This was the movement toward "freer" form, the goal being the creation of new open-ended procedures that allowed the improviser maximum control in shaping the ultimate form of a specific piece. The natural habitat for this type of experimentation was the small combo, the traditional medium for sympathetic interaction among individual performers and for individuality in general. Whereas the consequence of the experiments with preconceived forms and methods was to achieve a new intensity by adding substance and complexity to the musical structure — often at the expense of other considerations, the free form approach was an attempt to achieve the desired intensity by relaxing and simplifying the structure, thereby permitting and forcing the improviser to concentrate on other musical elements.

The word "freedom" appeared with regularity in published interviews with jazz musicians at the end of the fifties and in the early sixties. At that time many jazz musicians sought the emancipation from the dictates of the traditional jazz performance conventions. In doing so, they assumed greater responsibility and relied upon their own sense of discipline and personal taste. Reformer Cecil Taylor qualified the issue: "This is not a question of 'freedom' as opposed to 'nonfreedom,' but rather a question of recognizing different ideas and expressions of order."[8] The idea of order self-imposed by performers during the act of musical creation — order from within in contrast to that dictated by some external consideration such as a predetermined formal scheme or a predetermined chord progression — became the primary musical concern for a large number of jazz musicians.

The movement toward freer form was not a tendency peculiar to a certain faction of jazz artists or to jazz in general, but part of a greater movement "in science and philosophy as well as the arts — that tends to consider and express the world in terms of possibility rather than necessity."[9] In the recent art music of the European tradition, composers have introduced elements of chance and unpredictability into both the compositional and performance aspects of their music. This music, known as aleatory music, chance music, or music of indeterminacy, illustrates the freer form concept: "musical form and structure are no longer regarded as definitely fixed and final but as subject to partial or total transformation from one performance to another."[10] This goal was often realized by making compositional decisions — which pitches, their durations, and their distribution in time — on the basis of random selection. In addition, the idea of choice was introduced into the realization of the music by leaving some details and/or their order of appearance to the performer's discretion.

The Contributions of Charles Mingus

In jazz the details of a performance had always been subject to change. The structure of the majority of jazz pieces, however, had become predictable. Jazz exhibiting the relaxing of structure — of "form as possibility" — appeared in the several years before 1960 and became common in the years that followed. An important contributor to this development was Charles Mingus, string bassist and composer, whose activities anticipated many of the standard practices of the sixties. His compositional method was unusual in that the musicians of his band were directly involved in the compositional process. As early as 1956, Mingus described his methods in the following way:

> My present working methods use very little written material. I "write" compositions on mental score paper, then I lay out the composition part by part to the musicians. I play them the "framework" on piano so that they are all familiar with my interpretation and feeling and with the scale and chord progressions. . . . Each man's particular style is taken into consideration. They are given different rows of notes to use against each chord but they choose their own notes and play them in their own style, from scales as well as chords, except where a particular mood is indicated. In this way I can keep my own compositional flavor . . . and yet allow the musicians more individual freedom in the creation of their group lines and solos.[11]

The fact that Mingus nurtured performer choice and semicontrolled group improvisation is especially significant. His choice of the term "jazz workshop" as the designation for his ensembles was indicative of his attitude toward cooperative jazz composition.

Accompanying Mingus's approach to composition was his re-evaluation of traditional jazz schemes. By minimizing the theme-improvised variations-theme formula and by discarding the monothematic nature of most jazz pieces, he expanded the raw materials of jazz. In many Mingus compositions the principle of contrast became a function of musical structure. These works often suggest a suite-like character: a series of sections or movements differentiated by contrasting thematic material, mood, instrumentation and tone color, meter, or dynamics. The effect of his multi-sectional, multi-thematic conception is especially evident in his grand scale programmatic works. "Folk Form No. 1" on *Charles Mingus Presents Charles Mingus* (America AM–6082, 1960), "Reincarnation of a Lovebird" on *The Clown* (Atlantic 1260, 1957), and *The Black Saint and the Sinner Lady* (Impulse AS–35, 1963) illustrate Mingus's experiments with extended form.

The Adoption of Several Fixed Elements

One method for the relaxation of structural design involved the adoption of a small number of fixed elements for a specific piece. This assured the necessary musical coherence and allowed the performers to control the remaining parameters of the piece. The use of modal scales for improvisation was one manifestation of this practice. Ornette Coleman claimed to base his improvisations on his "impression" of a piece of music, not on the details of its harmonic or metric structure.

The most popular innovation of this variety was the adoption of a *basso ostinato,* a short melodic-harmonic unit of well-defined identity, as the basis for a piece of jazz. The unit was repeated throughout the duration of the piece, often arbitrarily determined by the musicians during the performance. It was varied and embellished by the rhythm section in a manner sympathetic to the character of the improvised solos, but its identity was not obscured. This procedure came to jazz from rock and roll where it was a standard structural device. In producing pieces of greater length and greater variety, a series of several ostinato patterns or an alternation of contrasting ostinato patterns were employed. The use of the *basso ostinato* in rock and jazz is similar to the chaconne bass or ground bass so popular during the Baroque Era of European fine-art music.

Examples of the use of the *basso ostinato* in jazz can be heard on *Forest Flower* by Charles Lloyd (Atlantic S–1473, 1967), *Journey in Satchidananda* by Alice Coltrane (Impulse AS 9203, 1970), and *A Tribute to Jack Johnson* by Miles Davis (Columbia CS KC–

30455, 1970). It was a common procedure in many pieces of rock-inspired jazz.

Free Group Improvisation

The ultimate venture in "free form" and in the practice of defining only a small number of musical parameters was free group improvisation, the act of qualified spontaneous creation of music by a group of sympathetic musicians. The participants contributed to the musical whole without the benefit of a common focus such as a preconceived composition. This music was necessarily flexible and irregular, and more than any other type of jazz, dependent upon its performers for cohesiveness and integrity.

The so-called jazz revolutionaries of the early sixties adopted the collective improvisation principle. This course of action represented a dramatic break with the historical mainstream of jazz because of the rejection of harmonic structures (chords and chord progressions), time structures (meter and constant pulse), and preconceived formal schemes (song forms, the blues, and variations). The contrapuntal nature of this music, the fitting together of the individual lines, became its most prominent feature in the absence of structurally important vertical reference points.

The subordination of the individual to the group, which must occur in free group improvisation, has been interpreted by Black Nationalists as symbolic of "the recognition among musicians that their art is not an affair of individual 'geniuses' but the musical expression of an entire people — the Black people in America."[12] White musicians involved in this facet of jazz did not need to subscribe to such a rationale. Blacks, however, were among the leaders in this sphere of activity.

The reappearance of collective improvisation[13] and the radical approach to jazz-making that accompanied it produced a series of shock waves within the jazz establishment, which met the innovation with cries of "anti-jazz." The development of collective improvisation, however, was closely related to many other less extreme modifications concurrent with it. Works that are characterized in part or entirely by the presence of free group improvisation are frequently based on some type of preperformance agreement, however minimal. Examples of free group improvisation may be found in "Folk Forms No. 1" by Charles Mingus on *Charles Mingus Presents Charles Mingus* (America AM–6082, 1960), *Free Jazz* by Ornette Coleman (Atlantic 1364, 1960), *Ascension* by John Coltrane (Impulse AS–95, 1965), and *Unit Structures* by Cecil Taylor (Blue Note 84237, 1966).

---

1   Nicolas Slonimsky, *Music Since 1900*, 4th ed. (New York: Scribner, 1971), p. 1497.

2   Whitney Balliett, *Dinosaurs in the Morning: Forty-one Pieces on Jazz* (New York: Lippincott, 1962), p. 214. Reprinted by permission of Harold Ober Associates Incorporated. Copyright © by Whitney Balliett.

3   Joe Goldberg, *Jazz Masters of the Fifties* (New York: Macmillan, 1965), p. 123.

4   John A. Tynan, "Stan Kenton's Neophonic Music," *down beat* 32 (January 14, 1965), 13.

5   *Ibid.*

6   In the liner notes for this recording, Hancock provides the following program: "The sea has often stirred the imagination of creative minds involved in all spheres of art. . . . This music attempts to capture its vastness and majesty, the splendor of a sea-going vessel on its maiden voyage, the graceful beauty of the playful dolphins, the constant struggle for survival of even the tiniest sea creatures, and the awesome destructive power of the hurricane, nemesis of seamen."

7   Stanley Dance, *The World of Duke Ellington* (New York: Scribner, 1970), pp. 260–61.

8   Nat Hentoff, "The Persistent Challenge of Cecil Taylor," *down beat* 32 (February 25, 1965), 17.

9   John Reeves White & André Boucourechliev, "Aleatory Music," *Harvard Dictionary of Music*, 2d ed., ed. Willi Apel (Cambridge, Mass.: Belknap, 1969), p. 27.

10   *Ibid.*

11   Balliett, *Dinosaurs in the Morning*, p. 102.

12   Frank Kofsky, *Black Nationalism and the Revolution in Music* (New York: Pathfinder, 1970), p. 140.

13   The New Orleans style of early jazz can also be appropriately described as a kind of collective improvisation.

Other Influences

South American and Caribbean musics, especially their rhythmic peculiarities, have always been matters of fascination to American jazz musicians. The results of another merger of transplanted European and African music as practiced by blacks in the New World, Latin American musics share common traits with jazz. Creole music was a major ingredient of the musical environment of New Orleans in the early days of jazz-making. The tango, a dance originating in Argentina, was accepted into American popular music in the early years of the twentieth century. In the late forties and early fifties, an Afro-Cuban fad swept popular culture in the United States. Elements of Afro-Cuban music, its percussion instruments and its dance rhythms, were accepted into the jazz idiom.

In the early sixties a variety of "samba jazz" known as the *bossa nova* reached popularity in the United States. The samba is a Brazilian dance genre of Afro-Brazilian origin, which developed in Rio de Janeiro and São Paulo after World War I.

> 'Samba' was a generic term designating, along with the *batuque*, the choreography of certain round dances imported from Angola or the Congo. The early folk samba presented some musical characteristics of Afro-Brazilian dances: it was in duple meter and rhythmically it revolved around the usual pattern ♪♩♩ , always stressing the strong beats. This was preserved in the urban version of the dance. The basic classical rhythmic formula used at first as accompaniment could have originated in the habanera rhythm, with the frequent addition of an accent syncopation on the second beat.[1]

The three classical samba rhythms as reported by Béhague are presented in Example 13.[2] Sixteenth-note pulsation and the dotted rhythm are characteristic features of the ostinato pattern. The urban samba became a popular ballroom dance during the thirties and forties and remained basically unchanged until the appearance of the *bossa nova*. A less sophisticated, but certainly more colorful and emphatic type of samba also existed and became particularly associated with the Carnival.

Example 13. Samba Ostinato Patterns

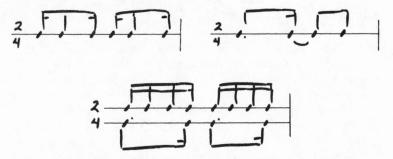

Three factors may be responsible for the acceptance of the *bossa nova* in American jazz circles. In the first place, the sound track to *Black Orpheus, Orfeu negro* (Epic LN–3672, 1960), a film that reached American audiences in 1959, was comprised of excellent examples of Brazilian popular music. António Carlos Jobim and Luiz Bonfá, composers of the score for the film, were leading figures in the *bossa nova* movement in Rio de Janeiro. Secondly, Laurindo Almeida, an outstanding Brazilian guitarist living in the Los Angeles area, and jazz saxophonist Bud Shank had been experimenting with blending elements of Brazilian music and jazz since 1953.

Probably more significant than either of these developments, however, was similar musical activity in Brazil, where urban musicians had nurtured jazz-like improvisations within a modified samba format since 1958–59. Vinícius de Moraes, the author of the play that later became the film *Black Orpheus*, credits António Carlos Jobim as the originator of the style.[3] The first major album exhibiting the new style, *Chega de Saudade* by João Gilberto (Odeon MOFB–3073, 1959), was based on a song of the same title by Jobim with lyrics by Moraes. Béhague attributes the development of the *bossa nova* to the "'internationalization' of style," an acceptance of elements of American jazz and Western popular music brought about by the collective taste of the rising Brazilian middle class.[4] Exposure to this genre of Brazilian popular music was the catalyst for the *bossa nova* epidemic in American jazz during the first half of the sixties.

The term "bossa nova," the Brazilian designation for this hybrid music, is Portuguese slang for the "new wrinkle" or the "new touch." The word "bossa" is also used to indicate a natural talent for music. Laurindo Almeida has confirmed this usage by reporting that its connotation to the musicians of Rio de Janeiro is "a good feeling for interpretation." For example, a musician may play with "a lot of bossa."[5] The first appearance of the term "bossa nova" occurred in 1959 in the lyrics to Jobim's well-known song "Desafinado."

Martin Williams defines the *bossa nova* as "the tension between a comparatively simple melody, with romantically unexpected intervals and twists, and an accompaniment in a contrastingly busy but flexible samba rhythm, lightly played."[6] The presence of the modified samba rhythm is indeed the single most distinctive feature of the *bossa nova*.

> The rhythmic structure of the *Bossa Nova* samba has its potential origin in both the folk and classical samba formula. João Gilberto was mainly responsible for extracting and isolating these elements that constitute his famous guitar stroke, called in Portuguese "violão gago", *i.e.*, stammering guitar.[7]

The rhythmic pattern established by Gilberto is given in Example 14.[8] Commonly used variants are provided in Example 15.[9] These *bossa nova* ostinatos should be compared to the samba rhythms illustrated in Example 13.

Example 14. Bossa Nova Pattern Established by Gilberto

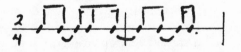

The prominent trait of these patterns is the presence of ternary groupings, represented by the dotted eighth note, within the framework of duple meter.

Both in Brazilian *bossa nova* and in its jazz adaptation, the literal repetition of the rhythmic unit as practiced in the traditional performance of the samba was abandoned. The units served a skeletal function, providing a point of departure for rhythmic variation. The melody and improvisations were superimposed upon this foundation. Both often contained references to the rhythmic formula or brought attention to it by deliberate contradiction in the form of consecutive eighth notes. Some musicians applied the unevenness of the swing concept to groups of eighth notes. Others performed consecutive eighth notes evenly allowing the built-in syncopations of the modified samba pattern to provide rhythmic vitality. This latter practice might be associated with a rhythmic quality identified in Brazil as *balanço*, an "oscillatory, swinging motion."[10]

Example 15. Variant *Bossa Nova* Rhythmic Formulas

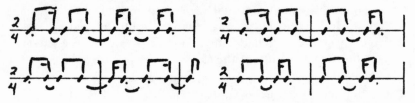

The guitar enjoyed a primary position in the performance of the Brazilian *bossa nova*. This became the situation in jazz performances also. The use of accessory percussion instruments, especially those of Afro-Brazilian origin, was another aspect of the imported practice imitated by jazz musicians. Eventually some jazz artists adopted the Brazilian custom of employing two drummers, one to deliver the characteristic rhythm and another to provide sympathetic variation to it.

The harmonic usage in the *bossa nova* was that of a lush chromaticism with frequent modulation. Harmonic patterns with frequent shifts between major and minor mode were favored. American jazz musicians, by the end of the fifties, were particularly well-disposed to improvise on such a harmonic foundation. The nostalgic lyricism of the melodies was also found attractive by exponents of the cool style. In addition, the structural design of samba tunes differed from American popular song forms. Many of these compositions exhibit a tripartite design and are cast in a harmonic structure of sixty-four measures. An interest in novel forms had already appeared among jazz musicians in the fifties.

Among the leading artists who became associated with "samba jazz" were saxophonists Stan Getz and Paul Desmond. It is a popular notion that white musicians resorted to the *bossa nova* because they were unable to identify musically and emotionally with the "blackening" of jazz that followed the heyday of the cool style. Although the generation of musicians who reached fame in the fifties did embrace the *bossa nova* movement in the early sixties, it would be misleading to assume that the genre held no attraction for black musicians who did not relate to the aesthetic goals of the cool style. Many black jazz musicians performed and recorded *bossa novas*.

All in all, the adaptation of the *bossa nova* by jazz artists, in spite of the superficial novelty of its "exotic" qualities, represented a continuation of traditional jazz methods. Because of the conventional and even conservative treatment of musical elements, it cannot be considered experimental or necessarily innovative. Nevertheless, the *bossa nova* enjoyed an immense wave of popularity. Many musicians well-known in Brazil became active in American jazz circles. Many *bossa nova* tunes, most notably the compositions of António Carlos Jobim, became part of the standard repertory of American jazz. A direct relationship between the popularity of the *bossa nova* and its acceptance into the heritage of jazz-making early in the decade, on the one hand, and the reappearance of "Latin" jazz in the early seventies, such as the efforts of Gato Barbieri, Chick Corea, Airto Moreira, and Don Ellis, on the other, is difficult to ascertain.

Representative recordings of the *bossa nova* in jazz are *Holiday in Brazil* by Laurindo Almeida and Bud Shank (World Pacific WP–1259, 1959), *Jazz Samba* by Stan Getz and Charlie Byrd (Verve 8432, 1962), *Getz-Gilberto* by Stan Getz, António Carlos Jobim, João Gilberto, and Astrud Gilberto (Verve 8545, 1964), *Bossa Antigua* by Paul Desmond (Victor LPM–3320, 1965), and *Rio* by Paul Winter (Columbia CS–9115, 1965). After the success of the *bossa nova* in the smaller jazz ensembles, it was adopted by arrangers for big bands. Examples of this development can be heard on *Big Band Bossa Nova* by Stan Getz with arrangements by Gary McFarland (Verve V–8494, 1962), *Bossa Nova* by Lalo Schifrin (Audio Fidelity AF–5981, 1962), and *Artistry in Bossa*

Nova by Stan Kenton (Capitol T–1931, 1963). The big-band context afforded, of course, more colorful instrumentation and orchestration and the harmonization of the poignant *bossa nova* tunes.

THE INCORPORATION OF ROCK

The assimilation of rock rhythmic patterns into jazz was another important addition to the diversity of styles within the jazz spectrum of the sixties. Rock and roll developed from a synthesis of black rhythm-and-blues and white country-and-western music, both commercial exploitations of folk expressions. The primary characteristics of rock and roll are the squareness of its rhythmic organization and the repetition of rhythmic patterns in ostinato fashion.

Bop musicians of the forties had modified jazz rhythm by making the sixteenth note the basic subdivision of their music and by minimizing the unequal stress of the eighth note, which had been codified in the large ensemble jazz of the preceding decade. In spite of the fact that the swing aspect was diminished, it never disappeared. The treatment of the eighth note in bop and cool can be viewed as a halfway point between swing and rock. The rhythmic practice in rock centers on the even subdivision of the beat — on "straight" eighth notes and "straight" sixteenth notes. Emphasis on beats 2 and 4, the "backbeat," is common, as is accentuation on the beat. Typical rock patterns, as illustrated in Example 16, emphasize the equal subdivision of the unit beats.

Example 16. Characteristic Rock Ostinatos

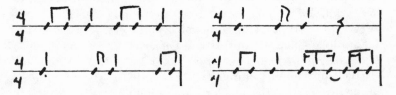

As jazz had developed, the timekeeping duties had been relegated more and more to the cymbals, especially the hi-hat, with rhythmic punctuation made with the snare drum and the bass drum. With rock and roll, there was a return to the earlier practice: the characteristic timekeeping was done by the drums; the cymbals were used as a means of accentuation. The reason for this change, perhaps, was the necessity in rock and roll for a definite attack by the timekeeper that could compete with the precise attack and volume level of the electric guitar. The vibrating sound of the cymbal was unsuitable for this purpose. Because of the importance of its timekeeping responsibilities and its role as the provider of metronomic ostinatos by which the rock rhythmic treatment is established, the drums became the cornerstone of the rock ensemble.

In its initial state in the late fifties, rock and roll was a trim, economical music, the unpretentious dance music of American youth. It exhibited fundamental chord progressions and relied upon the repetition of elementary rhythmic patterns in duple meter. It was a melody-oriented music in that its repertory consisted of songs with guitar, piano, and drum accompaniment. With the sixties, rock began the same process of romanticization that touched other popular musics. Its relative simplicity disappeared as much of its original musical vocabulary was elaborated, exaggerated, and sophisticated. The role of the Beatles in the expansion of the musical resources of rock in the mid-sixties was most influential. Although in most cases the Beatles were not the first to introduce new materials into rock, their ability to incorporate diverse elements into their music and to popularize them was exceptional. Throughout this evolution the importance of the drums in defining rock rhythmic practice and of the electric guitar, rock's basic coloristic feature, remained constant.

The movement toward a fusion of rock and jazz appeared in the second half of the sixties. Apparently by this time, enough common ground existed between the two that performers in one style could borrow elements from the other. This development took two forms: the activity of rock musicians adopting elements from jazz and the activity of jazz musicians adopting elements from rock.

Jazz Elements in a Rock Context

The influence of jazz on rock was the first to occur. This was possibly due to the arrival on the rock scene of well-trained and technically proficient instrumentalists who could no longer find satisfaction within the limitations of rock and roll. They sought to add substance to their music by emphasizing the instrumental aspect, by expanding possibilities for improvisation. Previously improvisation in rock had been restricted to short interludes and had been relatively unsophisticated because of the limited skills of "folk" musicians. The early solution to the problem of "jazz/rock" was the combination of a rock rhythm section and a jazz-oriented instrumental section. Music organized in this manner often exhibited the alternation of vocally-dominated composed sections and sections featuring solo instrumental improvisation, the presence of intricate instrumental riffs doubled in unison or harmonized in pandiatonic part-writing, the alternation of sections of contrasting tempo and meter, and the repetition of ostinato patterns.

Rock bands such as Blood, Sweat & Tears, Chicago, The Cream, Ten Wheel Drive, and Dream (all active in 1968 and 1969), were pioneers in this effort. Berendt points out that the formation of other groups modeled after these was often the result of the business goals of producers and recording companies rather than a sincere creative venture on the part of musicians.[11]

The chief consequence of jazz/rock was its impact on the big band. With traditional instrumentation and with its rhythm section functioning as a rock rhythm section, the big band became an enlarged version of the jazz/rock combo. The big bands of Buddy Rich, Thad Jones and Mel Lewis, Woody Herman, Maynard Ferguson, and Stan Kenton all adopted the procedures established by the smaller groups eventually.

An exceptional figure in the introduction of jazz elements into rock was Frank Zappa, whose music as performed by his ensemble The Mothers of Invention (founded 1964) revealed great craftsmanship and ingenuity. Zappa's musical background is one of the more interesting among jazz/rock musicians: he attended the *Kurse für Zeitgenössische Musik* in Darmstadt, Germany, in the fifties and heard lectures given by leaders of the European avant-garde; he enjoys close personal relationships with luminaries in the art-music circles of Los Angeles; and he has had first-hand experience in performing rock and jazz as an accomplished guitarist. The significance of Zappa as a composer and performer has been overshadowed by the social satire and bizarre humor that he has affixed to his music. This music is generally considered to be exemplary for its convincing fusion of rock, jazz, and fine-art elements.

Rock Elements in a Jazz Context

During the same period, a new generation of jazz musicians reached maturity. These musicians had grown up with rock and roll and had grown accustomed to its particular rhythmic energy. The music of black popular culture exerted a powerful influence on the musical goals of this younger generation of jazz musicians. The music of Jimi Hendrix, Sly Stone, B. B. King, Stevie Wonder, Aretha Franklin, and a host of other black rock musicians known collectively as the "Motown Sound" (because of their Detroit-centered recording company) was especially favored.

The sidemen of Miles Davis in the later sixties were the outstanding proponents of rock-influenced jazz. These men included Tony Williams (drums), Wayne Shorter (tenor saxophone), Joe Zawinul (piano), Chick Corea (piano), Herbie Hancock (piano), and John McLaughlin (electric guitar). With the assistance of these musicians, Davis stunned the jazz establishment in 1969 with the total integration of rock elements into his jazz concept in his recording *In a Silent Way* (Columbia CS–9875, 1969). In retrospect, it must be noted that this celebrated style change was not without warning; musical indications of the new direction appeared on several recordings prior to *In a Silent Way*. Two subsequent recordings by Davis, *Bitches Brew* (Columbia 2–GP 26, 1969) and *A Tribute to Jack Johnson* (Columbia CS KC–30455, 1970), solidified Davis's approach and established the standard for the incorporation of aspects of rock into jazz.

Davis's solution to the integration of rock features into jazz included the adoption of electronic instruments and devices, the underlying presence of complex multi-layered rhythmic ostinatos created by a complement of multiple percussionists and keyboard players, open-ended structures organized by the repetition of one or more ostinatos, solo improvisation as well as the group interaction of collective improvisation, and the use of modal scales. The single most constructive achievement was divising a system in which the rhythm section would not be "locked into" literal repetition of rhythmic patterns, but enabled to exercise the type of rhythmic freedom established in jazz earlier in the decade. Davis's music maintained the high level of volume that is associated with rock, but also a high level of musical abstraction, which is not associated with rock.

The trend established under Davis's leadership was reinforced by the activities of the alumni from his ensembles, activities begun in the late sixties and carried on well into the seventies. Recordings representative of these efforts are *Emergency!* by Tony Williams's Lifetime (Polydor 25–3001, 1970), *Birds of Fire* by John McLaughlin's Mahavishnu Orchestra (Columbia KC–31996, 1973), and albums by Joe Zawinul's Weather Report, Chick Corea's Return to Forever, and Herbie Hancock's ensembles. Weather Report and the Mahavishnu Orchestra became especially prominent in the seventies both as innovators and refiners of rock-inspired jazz and as popularizers of the new idiom.

Some observers viewed the resorting to rock elements by jazz musicians as a move to communicate with the listener on his own terms since rock music had captured the large audience. Others felt that avant-garde jazz earlier in the decade had lost touch with the listener and that the use of rock would lure the alienated back into the fold. The use of rock practices by jazz artists met with criticism from traditional and progressive forces alike who claimed that in doing so, musicians were "selling out" to commercial considerations. There may be some truth in each opinion. In any case the acceptance of rock elements into jazz broadened the financial base for the music, greatly increased its popularity, and set the direction for the early seventies. "In its jazz-rock form . . . it *is* the most successful jazz style since the Swing Era."[12]

---

1 Gerard Béhague, "Bossa & Bossas: Recent Changes in Brazilian Urban Popular Music," *Ethnomusicology* 17 (1973), 210.

2 *Ibid.*, 220.

3 Vinícius de Moraes, record liner notes to *Rio* by Paul Winter (Columbia CS–9115, 1965).

4 Béhague, "Bossa & Bossas," 211.

5 Robert Farris Thompson, "The 'Bossa Nova' from Brazil," *Saturday Review* 45 (September 15, 1962), 42.

6   Martin T. Williams, "Bossa from Both Sides of the Border," *Saturday Review* 46 (February 23, 1963), 57.
7   Béhague, "Bossa & Bossas," 213.
8   *Ibid.*, 221.
9   *Ibid.*, 222.
10   Béhague, "Bossa & Bossas," 213.
11   Joachim-Ernst Berendt, *The Jazz Book*, trans. by Dan Morgenstern, Helmut Bredigkeit, and Barbara Bredigkeit (New York: Lawrence Hill, 1975), p. 41.
12   Don Heckman, "Jazz-Rock," *Stereo Review* 33 (November 1974), 78.

Extra-Musical Connotations:
New Purposes

The notion that instrumental music can be strongly associated with rather specific non-musical information is a significant aspect of the legacy of Western music. The family of African-American musics, of which jazz is a prominent member, rightly belongs to this tradition in spite of its unique properties, and yet efforts to promote instrumental jazz as a means of communicating extra-musical ideas in any manner — suggestive or literal — remained a peripheral concern for much of jazz history. Nevertheless, an important body of jazz conceived during the sixties was generated as a method of expressing the idealism of the era, and, unlike their predecessors, many leading jazz figures of that decade assigned somewhat rigid meanings to their music. Although the compelling sociological and artistic circumstances surrounding this practice have passed, the music is best understood with its non-musical trappings fully noted.

HISTORICAL AND SOCIOLOGICAL BACKGROUND

A rather large repertory of music is commonly accepted as relating more to the listener than "organized sound" alone. In the fine-art tradition especially, particular generations of composers have embraced this idea wholeheartedly. The suggestion or representation of natural phenomena (e.g., water imagery, bird songs, sunrise, storms) through music is surely one of the oldest examples of this concept and certainly the most popular; it appears to be universal as well. Such musical correspondences have been accomplished by means of either the literal imitation of the sounds of nature (an objective approach) or their poetic evocation (a subjective approach).

During the nineteenth century, when the doctrine of Romanticism placed particular emphasis on pictorial representation through music and a union-of-the-arts ideal, a category of instrumental pieces known as program music dominated instrumental composition in the high culture of the West. Such pieces may be typically identified by the presence of descriptive titles rather than generic ones (Mussorgsky's *Pictures at an Exhibition* in contrast to Haydn's *Symphony No. 99 in E Flat Major*, for example). In many cases, composers supplied their listeners with conspicuous cues concerning "the program," be it a literary theme, a painting, a scene from nature, a particular mood, or a social cause. Many of these efforts, moreover, were related to the various nationalistic movements that spread throughout Europe and its cultural satellites in the wake of the French Revolution; patriotism and the matter of regional or ethnic identity became highly regarded (and popular) themes for musical treatment. Although many progressive composers of the fine-art tradition soundly rejected the concept of program music early in the twentieth century, the appeal and usefulness of the idea have lingered to the present day, most notably perhaps in filmscores.

Such an approach to instrumental music was slow to appear in the realm of jazz. This fact becomes completely understandable when the origins, purpose, nature, and milieu of jazz are considered. Because jazz began and remained, to a great extent, a manner of performing pre-existing pieces, the majority of jazz performances have been identified by the name of the "theme," commonly a popular song or dance tune. While it is true that original jazz tunes and compositions (e.g., the many versions of the blues) have always been assigned descriptive or fanciful names, an insistence that the music be linked in some meaningful way to non-musical ideas has remained exceptional. Social conditions institutionalizing the discrimination of blacks in the United States made it unfeasible or extremely difficult for black musicians to assign an overtly political message to their music, for example. The commercial performance context for jazz during the early decades of its existence also worked against such a practice. One might argue that the introduction of this dimension to the music would have been an unwelcome addition or an unnecessary complication to the entertainment setting.

After World War II, during the years witnessing the modern civil rights movement, the titles of a number of jazz pieces seem to have been given greater non-musical significance. These references appeared, however, without much commentary by musicians and without much reaction by the jazz public. During the sixties, with the temper of American society defined by social idealism and strongly influenced by black activism, jazz with programmatic associations achieved considerable prominence. In fact, through comments and writings, many jazz musicians proclaimed that their music and their music-making transmitted non-musical information.

As mentioned, there were noteworthy precedents that foreshadow this practice, although rarely was the extra-musical information presented in the crusading spirit of the sixties. A number of the novelty pieces of the Dixieland Era, for example several of the original compositions of Jelly Roll Morton, carry extra-musical associations. During the Swing Era, it became customary to name pieces based on the blues as well as original works (works not derived from a specific popular song) with colorful, descriptive titles. Many of Duke Ellington's creations for the Cotton Club were designed to express exotic locales and characters and are named accordingly. Likewise, the majority of his experiments with extended form — the so-called "tone poems" such as *Creole Rhapsody* (1931), *Black, Brown and Beige* (1943), *Deep South Suite* (1946), and *A Tone Parallel to Harlem* (1950) — bear a non-musical point of reference, at least by means of the title. The genre designation itself — "tone poem" — bespeaks a debt to nineteenth-century Romanticism. During the heyday of the bop rebellion, moreover, such titles as "Ornithology," "Now's the Time," and "Shaw 'Nuff," reflected the exclusionary agenda of young black musicians. The titles carried hidden meanings to insiders, just as only the initiated were fully aware of the unacknowledged source of the chord changes for many pieces. In general, however, such titles held few ramifications for the actual nature of the abstract music they identified.

During the years directly preceding the sixties, jazz titles assigned by black artists reflected a new spirit of racial confidence. In his summary of this trend between the years 1957 and 1961, Kofsky identified a representative sampling of titles as belonging to two categories: African-American themes and African themes.[1] His observations suggest that this development served as a prelude to the practices of the following decade, when certain streams of jazz became highly politicized and overtly programmatical:

> . . . taken en masse, these titles are strong evidence for the growth of (to use today's term) cultural nationalism among blacks. Though not explicitly either nationalist or political in nature, nonetheless, such works testify to the rising pride in blackness of Afro-American jazz artists.[2]

Although invoking African titles was largely symbolic in terms of the music, the glorification of African-American life was appropriately used to identify pieces affirming black American musical priorities, taking the blues and black worship music as points of departure in the so-called "funky" school of jazz.

During the sixties a rather dramatic change occurred. Many jazz musicians, including leading figures, routinely conceived and perceived their musical creations as more than objects of pure sound and subscribed to the belief that jazz can be a mode of expression capable of communicating far more than purely musical values. Indeed, in many instances, the new practice transcended the issue of program music in the conventional sense altogether, as numerous jazz musicians sincerely and emphatically associated their music-making with their own personal beliefs. The sixties proved to be a decade of frustration and searching, of re-evaluation and experimentation. Jazz musicians participated fully in both this intellectual quest and this "focus on feeling." Such a cultural climate nurtured jazz expression as a function of artistic, religious, social, and political convictions or as an aural analogue to these same ideas. In many cases, moreover, there was a blurring among these distinctions as jazz performances were intended to reflect the holistic worldview of the music makers. What stands as fundamentally important is the fact that the musicians presented their music in this manner and went to considerable lengths — notably elaborate liner notes on recordings and published interviews — to educate listeners to their intentions.

Of central importance to this practice is the attitude of musicians toward the music they produce, coupled with their attitude toward their own role in society. During the early decades of jazz, musicians tended to view themselves and to be viewed by others as skilled entertainers in the business of providing a commodity to certain sectors of the American public. Their music was functional in the sense that it was intended to accompany nightlife and party time; its value was determined as a sociological adjunct. As early as the late thirties, certain jazz musicians expressed resentment at being locked into this "servant" role. They insisted that their playing deserved to be accepted as a primary end in itself. Indeed, the music of bop artists was so intellectual, so highly abstract, that it could not be judged as anything but art. Progressive jazz musicians made the transition from good-time entertainers to musicians who sought to be accepted as artists. During the turbulence of the sixties this self-image was further enhanced. Jazz musicians began to understand their place in American society as one of serious cultural leadership and, accordingly, began to exercise the responsibility of educating, elevating, and even preaching to their audiences through music. As a result, their music took on added significance because of its extra-musical "content," its message. Prominent jazz musicians, like many rock and roll musicians and artists in various media responding to the same circumstances, assumed the responsibility of "high priests of culture" who instructed and nurtured society from individual perspectives.[3]

Three broad areas of practice relating to jazz and its extra-musical connotations during the decade may be identified: jazz as conventional program music, jazz as social protest, and jazz as religious expression. In any consideration of this topic, it is imperative to remember that, the presence of "a program" notwithstanding, good music must always stand on its own terms, that is, on musical terms. No matter how intricate or engaging a composer's or a performer's intention, his or her conception must work according to the rules of musical practice. At the same time, it is essential to acknowledge with some seriousness the creative artist's expressed sense of purpose to reach any balanced understanding of his or her contributions or achievements. Whether, indeed, extra-musical information is truly communicated by jazz is not the issue; what musicians believed they were communicating or what meaning they assigned to their music must be considered. During the sixties, as never before, jazz musicians advertised — often with a missionary's zeal, a propagandist's passion, or a poet's sensitivity — the extra-musical meaning they intended their music to communicate. The practice was not universally adopted, of course, but it did cut across the broad spectrum of jazz-making and, in retrospect, can be observed as one of the defining features of the period.

Jazz as Conventional Program Music

The appearance of jazz that exhibits the conventions of traditional program music may be readily explained as a borrowing from the fine-art tradition, where the idea has flourished. Its application at this particular time may be related to the emergence of jazz as concert music. Earlier in its history, jazz functioned as music for social dancing and as a background for informal entertainment. Bop musicians and their followers had chafed under these constraints and had eliminated social dancing to their performances by musical means, but were unable to remove their art from the context of the nightclub. In the fifties, through the example of the Modern Jazz Quartet and the success of the Dave Brubeck Quartet among others, jazz found a new home in the concert hall on a regular basis. (Many special jazz concerts had occurred earlier, of course, in such venues as Carnegie Hall.) On those occasions when the more formal setting replaced an informal atmosphere, the music and its performers became the unquestioned focus of attention. Ticket buyers paid to listen to the music — not to drink or to socialize. At the same time that jazz was admitting this "fine-art sensibility" into its sphere of performance customs, many of its leading spirits displayed an interest in certain ideas and procedures well established in the works of fine-art composers. In a number of these often self-conscious experiments, the emphasis on the calculated aspect — the element of composition — took a serious toll on the spontaneous aspect — the element of improvisation. In this climate, the appearance of jazz compositions cast as pieces of program music seems completely logical. The eventual addition of a program to specific pieces offered listeners a kind of relief to the highly sophisticated and often lengthy improvisations the musicians presented. There is little doubt that the majority of jazz musicians were fully familiar — either by formal training or self-study — with the standard concert repertory of the fine-art tradition.

The Celebration of Black America

It is no coincidence, perhaps, that a number of black jazz musicians in the sixties adopted the concept of program music as a means of paying homage to aspects of black life in America. In doing so, they were following in the footsteps of numerous nineteenth- and twentieth-century fine-art composers whose music had served to raise the social consciousness of an oppressed people. In the American fine-art culture, William Grant Still, for example, was a significant pioneer in this respect from the days of the Harlem Renaissance in the twenties. His programmatic *Afro-American Symphony* (1930), the first work in that form by a black American, is a masterful synthesis of European procedures and black American musical materials. Poetry by Paul Laurence Dunbar communicating the nobility of the black struggle was related to each movement of Still's symphony.[1] Some of Duke Ellington's compositions dating from these same years can be noted as a corollary development in the jazz tradition.

This type of expression in jazz was commonly designed in terms of an extended work, often a multi-movement suite for which the creator supplied the listener appropriate titles to guide the imagination. Each movement then represented a "character piece" whose subject was often indicated by a descriptive title. When such pieces were issued on recordings, liner notes devoted to a discussion of "the program" were often included. The performance medium was most frequently, but not necessarily, a large jazz ensemble with many orchestrational possibilities, either the traditional big band or a contemporary variant. Likewise, the role of the jazz musician as composer was usually quite prominent in such endeavors. The relationship between the fine-art orchestra and its repertory of symphonic poems and suites was obviously an influential model.

An important, early example of this category of jazz expression is "The Freedom Suite" by saxophonist Sonny Rollins. Recorded in 1958 with bassist Oscar Pettiford and drummer

Max Roach on the album *Freedom Suite* (Riverside OJC–067/ RLP–258, 1958), the piece represents Rollins's first work in extended composition and is a tour de force showcasing his improvisational skill. The nineteen minutes of uninterrupted music is cast as a chain of variations on a single theme, an old-fashioned formula by this time, but the soloist's variation technique and the contributions of his sidemen are so sophisticated as to belie the simplicity of the form. In addition to the title, what adds significance to this performance is Rollins's statement of conscience published on the record jacket:

> America is deeply rooted in Negro culture: its collo-quialisms, its humor, its music. How ironic that the Negro, who more than any other people can claim America's culture as his own, is being persecuted and repressed, that the Negro, who has exemplified the humanities in his very existence, is being rewarded with inhumanity.[5]

It is understood that a connection should be made between the music and this powerful declaration symbolized by the choice of title.

In his commentary on the album jacket, Orrin Keepnews tries to explain the novelty of this particular performance:

> For this is, as very few pieces of jazz writing even attempt to be, music *about* a specific subject. It is, by title, about "freedom," but just as that one word itself means many things, so does its application here have many facets. In most fields of music, a composition that is about something is concerned with a concrete picture, is "program music." But in jazz, which is so much a music of personal expression, "program music" is more fittingly about some*one*.[6]

Keepnews's point is interesting but somewhat misleading. It has indeed become customary to believe that African-American musics, because of the emphasis on improvisation and spontaneity in performance, constitute a more personal manner of expression than other kinds of music — a public mode of baring one's soul. It is not true, however, that the autobiographical element is absent in other kinds of program music. What tends to define program music is the presence of the expressed intent of the creator: the acknowledgement of a non-musical subject.

Keepnews's interpretation of the program of this piece, nonetheless, seems viable:

This suite, then, is "about" Sonny Rollins: more precisely, it is about freedom as Sonny is equipped to perceive it. He is a creative artist living in New York City in the 1950s; he is a jazz musician who, partly by absorbing elements of Bird and Monk and many others, has evolved his own personal music; he is a Negro. Thus the meaning of freedom to Rollins is compounded of all this and, undoubtedly, much more. In one sense, then the reference is to the musical freedom of this unusual combination of composition and improvisation; in another it is to physical and moral freedom, to the presence and absence of it in Sonny's own life and in the way of life of other Americans to whom he feels a relationship. Thus it is not a piece *about* Emmett Till, or Little Rock, or Harlem, or the peculiar local election laws of Georgia or Louisiana, no more than it is *about* the artistic freedom of jazz. But it *is* concerned with all such things, as they are observed by this musician and as they react — emotionally and intellectually — upon him.[7]

It is difficult, of course, to know precisely how Rollins's bold course of action as represented by "The Freedom Suite" influenced his musician peers, but it is clear that change was in the air. In spite of continuing pressures by the power structure to maintain the status quo, the political climate was changing markedly, and the possibility for jazz musicians to use their music for a new kind of social purpose was at hand. Rollins's album was reportedly recalled by the record company soon after its release and was fitted up with a much less controversial title — *Shadow Dance* — and a new censored jacket. New liner notes by Keepnews minimized the meaning of "The Freedom Suite," and the saxophonist's statement of conscience was omitted.[8]

Oliver Nelson's *Afro/American Sketches* (Prestige 7225, 1961), a jazz suite in seven movements for a large jazz ensemble (including four French horns and assorted percussion), conveys a similar purpose. Considering both the quality of the music and the rather specific nature of the program, it is an extraordinary example of this development. In rather extensive liner notes, the composer/saxophonist summarizes each movement in musical terms and sets forth the extra-musical theme suggested by each of the titles. The following details have been gleaned from his commentary (the capitalized words in his text indicate the title of individual movements):

> The MESSAGE relates that men in boats are coming up river in great numbers.

> JUNGLEAIRE is an account of a contest for freedom between the African Warriors and the slave traders. There is a contest in which the African loses, having been betrayed by some of his own people. He begins a new and more cruel existence in a world filled with hatred and bigotry.

> This [EMANCIPATION BLUES] is merely an attempt to depict what freedom must have meant to the American Negro when he was told, "You Are Free!" First he gives thanks, then celebrates the acquisition of his new liberties and then he wonders, "Free to go where, to do what?"

> THERE'S A YEARNIN', which in its entirety should read: There's A Yearnin' Deep Inside Me, is a lament. . . .

> GOING UP NORTH is a journey by the American Negro to make a better life, to live as a human being with rights, protection under the law and education for his children, he thinks.

> DISILLUSIONED opens with a beautiful cello solo . . . which tells us that the trip North for the Negro pioneer has proved little, that the Negro's position in society, politics, culture has not really changed. He realizes, however, if an individual has courage, patience and guts coupled with the will to overcome the hard knocks that go with being a Negro, social justice and the right to become somebody is at last within the realm of possibility.

> FREEDOM DANCE . . . is dedicated to the thousands of militant youths, Freedom Riders (of all races) and all people with the desire and maturity to be free. It is man's destiny to be free, free from want, sickness, oppression. In order to be really free though, man must first learn to respect the rights of other peoples, other cultures.[9]

Nelson has thus selected a series of moments in the history of American blacks for musical treatment. The range of feelings and moods corresponding to these subjects helps make his history lesson a dynamic musical experience.

Duke Ellington, who accepted responsibility as a black cultural leader for much of his career, may be represented during these years by his *New Orleans Suite* (Atlantic SD–1580, 1971). This eight-movement work constitutes Ellington's tribute to the musical milieu of New Orleans, the traditional "cradle" of jazz and, at the same time, becomes his tribute to the strong influence of musicians from New Orleans on the collective personality of his band and its repertory.[10] The music, though not as specifically descriptive as that found in the Nelson piece, is highly evocative. The composer provides specific cues for the listener with the following movement titles: "Blues for New Orleans," "Bourbon Street Jingling Jollies," "Portrait of Louis Armstrong," "Thanks for the Beautiful Land on the Delta," "Portrait of Wellman Braud," "Second Line," "Portrait of Sydney Bechet," "Aristocracy à la Jean Lafitte," and "Portrait of Mahalia Jackson." Each component of the suite serves as a musical vignette of the black heritage. Bass player Braud, clarinetist Bechet, and gospel singer Jackson had strong associations with New Orleans, but, interestingly, each of them also had significant associations with Ellington and his legendary band as well as Ellington's deepest admiration as musicians.[11]

The appearance of jazz pieces with programs calling attention to the indomitable spirit of black America — to Black Pride and Black Power, to use the mottos of the era — is, obviously, a contemporary response to the ongoing civil rights movement. In terms of both message and actual musical language, these pieces tend to explore a middle ground between an acceptance of the status quo and the radical experiments of the avant-garde. The musicians involved were, for the most part, well-established figures, not newcomers making a name for themselves. There were obviously a number of strategies adopted to heighten public awareness.

Expression of the Exotic and Other Romantic Topics

The subject matter of programmatic jazz was not limited, of course, to any one category. In fact, one might note another parallel with the fine-art tradition by pointing to "programs" that reflect a fascination with the exotic and other traditional Romantic topics. For example, the distinctive culture of the Iberian Peninsula always leaves indelible impressions on travellers. Miles Davis and Gil Evans joined countless musicians before them when they presented the recording *Sketches of Spain* (Columbia CL 1480, 1960), with its lush orchestral arrangements by Evans and its inimitable improvisations by Davis. Although "the program" is left largely to the imagination, the very title of the album invites the listener to receive its contents in the spirit of program music.

With the new awareness of non-Western cultures made manifest in the jazz world in various ways during the sixties, it is not surprising to find programmatic treatments of the Third World. Another extended work for Duke Ellington's band, *The Far East Suite* by Ellington and Billy Strayhorn (LPM/LSP–3782, 1966; reissued Bluebird 7640–1–RB, 1988), illustrates this exotic interest handsomely. The nine-movement composition owes its genesis to the 1963 tour of the Middle East and the Far East made by Ellington and his band under the sponsorship of the United States Department of State with a follow-up trip to Japan the next year. In a sense, it may be accepted as the jazz musician's counterpart to George Gershwin's symphonic souvenir *An American in Paris* or Aaron Copland's orchestral postcard *El salon Mexico*. The effect is the same: a geographic location and the memories of a tourist are communicated through the medium of music. What is ultimately distilled in the process are the musical personality of the composer and his musical perception of place. In the liner notes to the reissued version of this piece, Neil Tesser emphasized this point:

> Despite his fanciful emendation of the world map, though, Ellington's sense of musical geography proved stunningly accurate. Has anyone ever captured a locale so completely — with music so clearly tethered to the place in questions — and yet remained so much himself? Each segment of the *Far East Suite* is typically, unmistakably Ellington, using colors, rhythms, melodic contours he had pioneered nearly four decades earlier, buoyed by the familiar, barely reined energy of his close-knit orchestra. Yet at the same time each segment stands as a brilliant example of musical journalism, conveying the scene and story, the fascinating flavors and unfamiliar aromas, through the sensibilities of a terrific reporter.[12]

Ellington provided the record jacket annotations for the initial release of the recording; in addition, his autobiography, *Music Is My Mistress* (1973), contains a chapter titled "Notes on the State Department Tour, 1963," which offers further commentary on this experience.[13] In characteristic fashion, moreover, the title of each movement helps the listener follow Ellington's musical travelogue: "Tourist Point of View," the excitement of arrival in a foreign place; "Bluebird of Delhi (Mynah)," based on a birdsong heard in India; "Isfahan," the memory of a city in pre-revolutionary Iran, where, according to Ellington, "everything is poetry"; "Depk," inspired by a children's dance in Amman, Jordan; "Mount Harissa," a hilltop outside of Beirut, Lebanon, marked by an imposing statue of Our Lady of Lebanon (the spiritual and musical centerpiece of the suite); "Blue Pepper (Far East of the Blues)," the clash of East and West; "Agra," an evocation of the Indian city and its famous Taj Mahal; "Amad," a general overview of the Middle East; and finally "Ad Lib on Nippon," an evocation of Japan.

The interest in other traditional themes, in this case the mysteries of nature, is represented by the album *Maiden Voyage* by pianist Herbie Hancock (Blue Note BLP–4195/84195, 1965), a collection of five pieces depicting sea scenes. On the record jacket, Hancock directs the listener's imagination:

> The sea has often stirred the imagination of creative minds involved in all spheres of art. There still exists an element of mystery which surrounds the sea and the living aquatic creatures which provide it with its vital essence. Atlantis, the Sargasso Sea, giant serpents, and mermaids are only a few of the many folkloric mysteries which have evolved through man's experiences with the sea.
> This music attempts to capture its vastness and majesty, the splendor of a sea-going vessel on its maiden voyage, the graceful beauty of the playful dolphins, the constant struggle for survival of even the tiniest sea creatures, and the awesome destructive power of the hurricane, nemesis of seamen.[14]

As if Hancock's observations were not sufficient, the remainder of the liner notes is devoted to Nora Kelly's detailed narrative, entitled "Maiden Voyage." This text, reprinted here to document the importance some musicians placed on the extra-musical aspect of the music, calls forth powerful images of the sea.

Before the dawn the water is clear and quiet, the small movement of the waves so rhythmic it is a stillness in itself. The birds are silent, and the beach is as empty as the sky, except for a few small crabs that poke among the rocks, looking for food tinier than they.

As the first hint of gray suffuses the horizon and imperceptibly lightens the deep black waters, a light wind ruffles the tips of the wavelets, whitening their crests with tongues of foam. Slowly the sand gains life, the grayness of the starry night becoming faintly yellow, a forerunner to the blazing white of noon.

In this empty hour the busy world is shrouded in loneliness. Half-buried beer cans glint weakly in the diffused light, and as the day grows broader, the whole length of the beach slowly becomes visible, vast and silent, the discarded residue of humanity scarring its desert purity. Metal wastebaskets are dotted over the landscape as far as the eye can see, looking strange and useless, as desolate as gravestones.

A single ship, perhaps on her maiden voyage, her mast a black spike against the sky, hovers near the horizon, until the curving waters sink her sail from view. The sand twinkles in the growing day, but all too soon the sea will break on a shore of people. Gone will be the huge, secret silence, as the masses stream from the city behind, scurrying madly like lemmings to the waiting strand.

But though the land may submit, the sea is yet implacable, changeless, and though the people, deeming themselves brave, tiptoe out from the edge of the land and splash in the shallows, tasting the salt, they can but shiver on the fringes of her mystery. Her vastness remains dark and secret, a misty world of silence and beauty and fluid grace. From the great sluggish sea turtles gliding in slow motion through the depths, to the swift and playful dolphins, jesters and intelligentsia of her kingdom, everything in the sea moves constantly in flight or pursuit.

To us a playground or a symbol of peace, to her creatures the sea is a watery jungle, a world of swift life and swifter death, whose silence cloaks a lurking danger. Killer whales, cruel kings of the sea, cruise slowly about, slaying for the love of blood and battle. Sea anemones, beautiful and deadly, wave their tentacles, beckoning small fish to death by poison. Like the land, it is a world where the small and timid must be swift and clever at hiding, where the strong prey on the weak, the weak on those more defenseless than themselves, a world where only the fittest survive.

Ancient tales speak of its beauty and danger, of nameless terrors that lurk in the shadows, awaiting the unwary, of fantastic monsters rearing vast and hideous heads from the depths, crunching ships in two with one snap of their jaws.

They speak too of the wondrous cities built by men of old under the sea, that appear only once in a hundred years, only to sink beneath the surface again, leaving no trace. Yet in truth, no cities of man exist beneath the sea, and lost Atlantis is but a woman's tale. The sea yet holds her secrets, and it will be many a long year ere man plumbs her depths, ravaging her beauty, imprisoning her creatures, usurping her throne with a savage hand.[15]

Four of the five pieces on the album carry titles directly related to this prose: "Maiden Voyage," "The Eye of the Hurricane," "Little One," "Survival of the Fittest," and "Dolphin Dance." Hancock's quintet includes Freddie Hubbard, trumpet; George Coleman, tenor saxophone; Ron Carter, bass; and Tony Williams, drums.

Another fine effort, with obvious similarities to Hancock's *Maiden Voyage*, is *Odyssey of Iska* by saxophonist Wayne Shorter (Blue Note 84363, 1970). This album, consisting of a suite of five performances by Shorter backed by a double rhythm section, represents, in his own words, "a pictorial-musical journey symbolizing the lifetime and whatever happens after."[16] In addition, the soloist instructs the listener about the provenance of the name "Iska" and its significance: "Iska . . . is the wind. It's like a breeze that comes and goes without leaving any trace. It's Nigerian — not exactly a Nigerian word, but a poetic expression. It represents the transition of each man's soul as it passes through life . . ."[17] To make the extra-musical content even more emphatic, the listener receives with the recording what may be regarded as either an explanation of the music or a prose companion to it prepared by Shorter. The text is duplicated here:

Iska is the wind that passes, leaving no trace . . .

Imagine — the wind having been born with a formless soul that travels through time and space — with a life of its own; seeking life, encountering the realities and fantasies of man and his endless journey — the wind — so vast in scope, so boundless as to suggest infinity in absolute form — taking all that exists, (past, present and future), on a once in a lifetime odyssey . . .

Perhaps you can relate the enclosed [the music] to the journey of your own soul; your body serving as the ship's hull, weathering the barriers of ignorance, hate, greed and other known evils, (hang ups, drags — whatever). Fortunately, Iska does not linger, like a brooding defeatest wringing dry the self-pity rational, until stagnation sets in as a prelude to final decay! Fortunately, Iska fights with the ferocity of a wild boar; surrendering only to the urge to move on, altering its future . . . leaving no tracks —

A storm speaks for itself . . . you won't need much to imagine a storm — but whatever a storm needs to be one — imagine! Adversity! Pig-headedness! Antagonism at it's worst [*sic*] . . . known and unknown fears . . . an evil world's mind polluted people — when the storm reaches its meanest, there isn't time to pray! Meanwhile, there's the serpent's shadow; threatening, challenging, demanding submission — unconditional and total denial of faith and belief in the good design for resurrection and salvation . . .

Now, a great being descends upon the face of Iska bringing all confusion, turmoil and chaos to a gentle halting which settles with the contentment of calm, that pause which is so necessary when God speaks . . . to know one is not alone . . .

"To know God is to know one is not alone

To know one is not alone is to know woman." Earth, flower, sun, water. They live linked in a rhythm every so steady — one feeding the other, helping passengers to survive on terra firma. After the hate, the war, the greed and the ignorance have all been used, what is there left for food? Might not there be time left for one to love another without draining that magic from its source? (De Pois Do Amor, O Vazio.) What Iska could tell us about the nature of love would be better left untold. A man called Jesus has spoken strongly on the subject of love: poets, philosophers and playwrights all had their say . . . anything added here would seem superfluous —

And then there's that elusive thing . . . you travel on and on. It takes a while to get there; some try during a lifetime and never quite arrive . . . some try to manufacture it in one form or another; the manifestations of which, are often shattering! Holidays, church sermons, drugs, mass entertainment perhaps all lead to some temporary feeling of happiness — but to arrive at something more is where the wind wants to go . . . some call that place — joy! Some find it with companions . . . some find it alone. Can't weigh it or measure it — you do it . . .

With Iska, that something more is all the joy anyone ever experienced. Iska knows there is no possessing joy —

the person who finds it alone should be able to give to someone else with great ease — the enclosed [music] speaks of
such generosity . . . let us speak of joy — happiness —
exultation!
    Let us speak of music . . . it is as all things are, a necessary
indulgence — to give food and sustenance to the travelers
as they move on through all their odysseys.
    Iska is the wind that passes; leaving no trace . . . [18]

No matter the critical assessment of the prose, this essay is striking. Taken on its own terms, it can be understood as addressing
a variety of the key cultural themes of the decade: the search for
individual meaning and personal happiness in an inhospitable
environment; a zest for hedonistic recreation; an emphasis on
ecstatic emotional states; and a religious point of view no longer
limited by the Judeo-Christian ethic, but receptive as well to the
spiritual values of non-Western societies. In the broader sense, it
is equally memorable. In essence, Shorter argues that this music
is conceived to communicate a similar philosophical content presented in the genre of the symphony by a line of distinguished
fine-art composers dating from Beethoven at the beginning of
the nineteenth century — the struggle of humanity to endure!
Shorter's musical language and formal approach are, naturally,
markedly different from those of Beethoven and his descendents, but the expressed purpose of the music is indeed compa-
rable. The nature of this "odyssey," cast in the sensual and eclectic
style of much late sixties' jazz, is re-enforced by the progression of
movements: "Wind," "Storm," "Calm," "De pois do amor" [After
Love, Emptiness], and "Joy."

Jazz with Poetry

    As the decade of the sixties unfolded, it became increasingly
common for jazz musicians to join their music with other art
forms such as poetry or dance. When a piece of jazz was allied to
a poem, the poet was often one of the performers. Among such
poet-musicians were Sun Ra, Cecil Taylor, Yusef Lateef, Archie
Shepp, and John Coltrane. This interest in poetry was different from the relationship between jazz and poetry during the
fifties when the so-called Beat poets idealized jazz improvisation for its "stream-of-consciousness" honesty and modeled their
own poems after it. In the sixties, jazz musicians, attempting to

heighten the musical experience, chose to compound the artistic stimuli through additional means of creative communication. At least two strategies can be recognized: associating a poem with a particular jazz piece in the spirit of program music and delivering a poem in the course of a jazz performance. In the first instance, the listener was guided to consider specific thoughts and images. In the second, the musicians often specified an unequivocal meaning for individual compositions or performances. By imposing a poem on top of the music in performance, they went a step beyond providing cues to the listeners: the message became explicit, undeniable!

The former practice is well demonstrated by the Dave Brubeck Quartet's *Jazz Impressions of Japan* (Columbia PC 9012, 1964), a collection of eight "personal impressions" from a 1964 tour of Japan. Brubeck describes the purpose of the music-making as an attempt "to convey these minute but lasting impressions, somewhat in the manner of classical haiku, wherein the poet expects the reader to feel the scene himself as an experience. The poem only *suggests* the feeling." [19] Accordingly, each piece on the album is assigned a programmatic title; the significance of the individual titles is explained by Brubeck in the liner notes in terms of the Quartet's experiences in Japan; and a haiku poem by a recognized Japanese master poet is paired with each piece to convey the emotional essence of each specific experience documented by music. Thus, the listener is given three non-musical aids to enhance the musical perception. Brubeck's preparation of the listener for "Fujiyama" and the accompanying poem by Issa may serve as an illustration of this procedure:

> For centuries artists have painted Mount Fuji as the soul of Japan. Flying along Fuji-san on our way to Nagoya, it was evident that the majesty of this awesome mountain had not been exaggerated. I tried to imagine a pilgrimage up the slope of Fuji and wrote a pastorale-like theme, *Fujiyama*.

> 'The snail does all he can
> But oh, it takes him quite a while
> To climb great Fuji-San.'
>
> ISSA [20]

The Oriental subject of these pieces and the affectations of Oriental practice (parallel fourths and fifths, for example) in the music are further indications of the appeal of exoticism during the sixties. In this case, musicians such as Brubeck and saxophonist Paul Desmond, who must be judged as conservatives, are participating in the times according to their own lights.

The album *The Lowlands* (Fantasy 86018, 1969) by saxophonist Archie Shepp and drummer Philly Joe Jones provides two provocative examples that unite jazz and poetry according to the second strategy. The poetry pertaining to each appears on the record jacket and is recited during the musical performance. According to poet and composer, Chicago Beau (L. T. Beauchamp), who also participates as an instrumentalist (soprano saxophone and harmonica), the performance of "The Lowlands" represents

> a musical portrait of life in the black ghettos and southern black communities. The music begins with shouts and screams because shouts and screams are a sure sign of life. Whether one is shouting for joy or screaming in pain life and feeling for whatever is expressed here.[21]

Moreover, he characterizes Shepp's tenor solo as "a tour of the Lowlands which hopefully is an unforgettable one" and calls the background provided by the supporting musicians "interesting, mad, black, wild."[22] The piece ends in a series of anguishing screams. The brief poem, which shares its title with the piece and the album, addresses the realities of black life in America without much elaboration, thereby allowing the music to serve as a powerful subtext.

```
The Lowlands,
     a place,
                 made up of,
          screams
          shouts !
                    music
                      life.


     The Lowlands
          home
          of
               all the brothers
          ghetto people !
          free spirited
                    happy
                    in the
          LOWLANDS.
```
[23]

The companion piece on this album, "Howling in the silence," is a composition by Julio Finn with poetry by Augustus Arnold. Once again the composer takes the opportunity to explain the extra-musical content of the work:

> "Howling in the silence" is a love song and utilizes a love poem which aptly explains the difficulties anyone has when trying to express a feeling so deep that he may wonder if he has ever felt it before. . . .
> What is "howling in the silence"? Examples, I think, are the best explanation: Charlie Parker, Billie Holiday, John Coltrane, Martin Luther King. I have used this expression because I think it is the most beautiful way to say "screaming."[24]

Arnold's poem is entitled "These Little Things":

> What I have   - I don't want.
> What I want   - I can't have;
> What is   - isn't worth it.
> What isn't   - cost too much.
> The woman I love   - loves another man.
> The other man - perhaps he's me, hiding.
> The things I love   - are avoiding me.
> Yet these things make the days worthwhile.
> Little things like this:
> What I say - any fool can holler.
> What I would like to say - cannot be said.[25]

These illustrations clearly indicate that musicians adopting this progressive multi-media approach devoted themselves to serious, high-minded themes. For many, the idea of jazz offered as musical entertainment, either frivolous or sophisticated, had been superseded by high artistic goals that would have been foreign to jazz musicians performing in the earlier decades of the twentieth century. Examples by Archie Shepp and John Coltrane are described later in this chapter. The discussion to follow amplifies the relationship of many such works to the social dilemma confronting black Americans.

JAZZ AS SOCIAL PROTEST

Of critical importance to any study of jazz is a consideration of the general temper of the black community in the United

States. The social tensions between American blacks and the white establishment came into sharper focus during the sixties as a result of the redefinition of attitudes by blacks and the increased activism that accompanied it. The attempt by blacks to assimilate into the mainstream of white society, although constantly challenged by significant black leaders throughout the twentieth century, was ultimately rejected as a futile strategy by many black citizens as the civil rights movement reached its peak in intensity during the sixties. In the wake of favorable Supreme Court rulings, the quest for integration was modified in some quarters, but the insistence on equal opportunity under the law was widely accepted as both a rallying cry and as a fundamental goal. Blacks organized themselves into powerful social and political forces. Although Dr. Martin Luther King, Jr., was the most prominent among black leaders, no single individual gained the universal allegiance of black people, and no one unifying organization assumed command of their agenda. There was, nonetheless, an undeniable common effect: a renewal of identity for black Americans bolstered by a new sense of pride and self-worth. The sit-ins, demonstrations, boycotts, marches, and riots successfully jarred the consciousness of the mainstream society and challenged the system of institutionalized segregation to the point that true progress in granting civil rights to black Americans—rights guaranteed by law, but ignored by social convention and law-enforcement—was made.

The Rise of Black Nationalism

In a sense, the search for a new black identity and the dynamic methods employed to achieve it may be likened to a movement for nationalism — the struggle of an oppressed people for social, economic, and psychological independence.[26] The cause of nationalism is fostered by developing symbols, heroes, and cult figures, and, of course, by cultivating artistic expression. During these years black Americans adopted a number of mannerisms intentionally designed to call public notice to their alienation from white America: the Black Power fist (used to great advantage by black athletes at the 1968 Summer Olympics in Mexico City), a characteristic greeting ritual among young males, clothing styles and fabric designs proclaiming African origins, the rejection of slavemaster names in favor of African or Muslim names, decals recalling the "Back to Africa" movement of Marcus Garvey of the twenties, a new respect for black dialect and slang, and the celebration of a quality supposedly exclusive to blacks — soul.[27] The term "soul" gained special currency in jazz during the late fifties as a means of identifying the black reaction to the cool style (a back-to-basics affirmation of black musical priorities) and was reused during the sixties to designate the stream of black popular music that championed the use of the blues. In both cases, in part because of the spiritual connotations of the term "soul," the emotional and musical debt to the black Protestant Church is appropriately acknowledged. The slogan "Black Is Beautiful" burst forth as one of the most powerful messages of the era.

The response by American blacks to the positive values of their own history was at the heart of this movement. Before the activism that culminated in the sixties, it had been the custom in America for history to be interpreted from the point of view of the mainstream white culture when dealing with subjects concerning minority elements in society. Historical studies written from the black point of view began not only to be published, but to reach a considerable audience.[28] The accomplishments and contributions of black men and women to American culture and to humanity in general, as well as accounts of earlier African civilizations, became accessible to American blacks as never before and, in effect, offered them the meaningful roots that white society had traditionally ignored. The remarkable influence on American blacks of the newly won mantle of history caused Imamu Amiri Baraka (formerly LeRoi Jones) to declare proudly in 1963: "The idea of the Negro's having 'roots' and that they are a valuable possession, rather than the source of ineradicable shame, is perhaps the profoundest change within the Negro consciousness since the early part of the century."[29]

As noted earlier, the conditions facing the black community spawned a broad range of organized responses and an outpouring of feelings. At the far end of the spectrum stood those who had reached an unforgiving attitude toward the struggle at hand. The most controversial and most militant among these groups — the ones most threatening to the white establishment — included the Black Panthers (founded in 1966 and based in Oakland, California), an organization whose members advocated self-defense by whatever means necessary, including violence, and the Nation of Islam or Black Muslims, a religious sect loosely connected with the Moslem faith.[30] A basic tenet of the Black Muslims is the premise that self-respect and self-sufficiency for blacks can only be realized by a self-imposed separation of the races. The latter organization was particularly successful in recruiting members — jazz musicians among them — during the emotional tumult of the sixties and reached its peak in membership and influence during that decade.

Perhaps the most influential and uncompromising figure in the cause of Black Nationalism was Malcolm X (formerly Malcolm Little).[31] As the electrifying spokesperson of Elijah Muhammad, he crusaded among American blacks expounding the separatist doctrines of the Nation of Islam. In time, however, Malcolm X took issue with the non-aggressive nature of the sect and dissociated himself from the Black Muslims. Having been converted to orthodox Islam in 1964, he continued to work for the cause of Black Nationalism until assassins gunned him down at a Harlem rally in 1965. Malcolm X fearlessly and emphatically charged that the white establishment was responsible for all previous and contemporary ills and inequalities suffered by blacks. He was prepared to right this situation by social revolution and did not preclude the possibility of violence. When confronted with the observation that "he was the only Negro in America who could either start a race riot — or stop one," he replied, "I don't know if I could start one. I don't know if I'd want to stop one."[32] He deprecated any form of compromise with white society and criticized those blacks willing to compromise almost as severely as he reviled his white opponents. Near the end of his life, after achieving an international reputation, he supported the bonding of non-whites around the world — especially American blacks and Africans — as a constructive force in dealing with injustice and moved toward cooperation with the mainstream of the civil rights movement in the United States.

Although Malcolm X was branded as an "ambassador of hatred and reverse racism" by his enemies, his honesty and courage provided an important model for all blacks. Ultimately he became a martyr for their cause. His influence on black musicians, especially the generation making itself known during these tempestuous times, was profound.[33] The title of saxophonist Archie Shepp's posthumous musical tribute to him, "Malcolm, Malcolm — Semper Malcolm" from the album *Fire Music* (Impulse AS–86, 1965), may be perceived as an attempt to underscore this strong association. The impact of Malcolm's life, moreover, continues to be felt by some contemporary black jazz musicians. In a 1989 interview in *down beat* magazine, almost twenty-five years after the assassination, saxophonist Greg Osby acknowledges the importance of Malcolm's speeches in forming his own work ethic and career goals.[34]

A kindred spirit to Malcolm X was the playwright and poet Imamu Amiri Baraka [formerly LeRoi Jones]. Baraka, a major force in African-American and American letters and a political activist of no small influence, adopted his "Pan-African-Islamic-warrior" designation in 1967.[35] This new name, which means "Blessed Prince" in Arabic and is pronounced according to African (Bantu-Swahili) practice, represented for him a transformation into "a blacker being."[36] Baraka is an especially significant figure because he articulated and publicized the militant point of view in various arenas and served both as a foremost spokesperson for the black avant-garde in jazz during the sixties as well as an unapologetic, uncompromising defender of its members. He has written extensively on the subject of black music and is widely known for highly controversial opinions. Particularly relevant is Baraka's formulation and dissemination of an aesthetic view that explains and justifies many aspects of the black avant-garde in jazz. This view, derived at least in part from the functional nature of African art, has been summarized by one scholar in the following manner: "art forms, like history itself, evolve as organic modes that exemplify the [artist's] perception of experience as an inviolable whole; and in turn that sense of cosmic wholeness is reenforced by the integration of history and art."[37] According to Baraka's worldview, jazz must inevitably reflect the social consciousness of blacks and must function as a form of social protest.[38]

There were, of course, many contributors to the complex fabric of African-American culture during these especially exciting years when Black America demanded its own identity and embraced the politics of confrontation as never before. The roles of Malcolm X and Baraka have been emphasized in this discussion because of their special relationship to those jazz musicians who used their music in the militant crusade for identity and opportunity.

The Position of Young Black Musicians

For many black musicians during the sixties the act of playing jazz became a meaningful testimonial, a sincere form of protest and defiance that was, at the same time, personal, social, and artistic.[39] Although the human feelings motivating such behavior did not originate with this generation of performers, such expression through jazz represented a conscious break with the past, a notable departure from tradition.

Black musicians have always been understood as a special symbol of the black American identity: their music has always been perceived as a light illuminating the black experience in America.[40] This was the case in spite of widespread exploitation of black musicians by the mainstream entertainment industry and in spite of the general pattern of imitation by white musicians. In his history of black music in America, Baraka describes the relationship between music and the black experience as fundamental:

> I think it is not fantastic to say that only in music has there been any significant Negro contribution to *formal* American culture. . . . Only Negro music, because, perhaps, it drew its strength and beauty out of the depths of the black man's soul, and because to a large extent its traditions could be carried on by the "lowest classes" of Negroes, has been able to survive the constant and willful dilutions of the black middle class and the persistent call to oblivion made by the mainstream of the society.[41]

For all practical purposes, the structure of the jazz world that had evolved in the United States up until that time may be described by the analogy of an imperialistic power and its colony. With minor exceptions, whites controlled the economic interests: the night clubs, the booking agencies, the recording companies, the radio stations, the festivals, and the jazz periodicals. The critics, who exerted untold influence, were also in most cases white. Although individual whites who worked in this empire, especially the musicians, were often sincerely sympathetic to the black cause, the apparent segregation of management and worker made black musicians likely candidates for some form of activism. Their point of view, as expressed by Archie Shepp, was, "You own the music and we make it." [12]

Many jazz artists, accordingly, participated in the forefront of the movement for Black Nationalism. Angry young black musicians tended to accept and espouse a number of specific, highly controversial conclusions concerning the nature of jazz and its history. The following manifesto was considered in the pages of *down beat* magazine in 1966:

> 1. Only Negroes can play great jazz.
>
> 2. All the originators in jazz, the truly creative jazzmen — the innovators — were and are Negroes.
>
> 3. Jazz is Negro protest music that only Negroes and a few whites infused with something of a "black" outlook can understand and appreciate.
>
> 4. All Negroes in jazz have been, and are now being, exploited by whites and the "white power structure." [13]

Such an interpretation of historical fact and contemporary problems along racial lines was unquestionably and, perhaps intentionally, self-serving. The times required that the subject be treated in a sensational, propaganda-like manner. With some qualification, a factual basis for these assertions exists, but such an intolerant explanation also contributes to a distortion of history. In retrospect, the extreme nature of these "battle cries" suggests a form of deliberate overcompensation — as if the time-honored tradition of injustice could only be rectified by shocking tactics.

The eloquent, if intentionally menacing, writings of saxophonist and playwright Archie Shepp indicate the tenor of the rhetoric of militant black jazz musicians:

> The Negro musician is a reflection of the Negro people as a social phenomenon. His purpose ought to be to liberate America aesthetically and socially from its inhumanity. The inhumanity of the white American to the black American, as well as the inhumanity of the white American to the white American, is not basic to America and can be exor-

cised. I think the Negro people through the force of their struggles are the only hope of saving America, the political or cultural America.

Cultural America is a backward country; Americans are backward. But jazz is American reality — total reality. . . . Some whites seem to think they have a right to jazz. Perhaps, that's true, but they should feel thankful for jazz. It has been a gift that the Negro has given, but [whites] can't accept that — there are too many problems involved with the social and historical relationship of the two peoples. It makes it difficult for them to accept jazz and the Negro as its true innovator.[44]

Jazz in the service of Black Nationalism effected a dramatic means of expressing social doctrines and the emotional disposition of its adherents. Nurtured on the examples of Charles Mingus, Max Roach, John Coltrane, and Archie Shepp, a generation of outspoken black jazz musicians emerged and made its mark by "using . . . music as an eloquent vehicle for a consciousness of self in America."[15]

This attitude — this insistence on the extra-musical meaning in jazz — and the awareness that it represented something new in black music can be documented by numerous performances from the period. In the liner notes to an especially important collection of avant-garde performances entitled *The New Wave in Jazz* (Impulse A–90, 1965), Steve Young provides an introduction that cites both the anger and the hope played into the improvisations:

Here then is the music of a new breed of musicians. We might call them "The Beautiful Warriors" or witch doctors and ju ju men . . . astro-scientists, and magicians of the soul. When they play they perform an exorcism on the soul, the mind. If you're not ready for the lands of Dada-Surreal à la Harlem, South Philly and dark Georgia nights after sundown, night-time Mau Mau attacks, shadowy figures out of flying saucers and music of the spheres, you might not survive the experience of listening to John Coltrane, Archie Shepp or Albert Ayler. These men are dangerous and someday they may murder, send the weaker hearts and corrupt consciences leaping through windows or screaming through their destroyed dream worlds. But this music, even though its speaks of horrible and frightening things, speaks at the same time so perfectly about the heart and to the

123

heart. This music, at the same time it contains pain and anger and hope, contains a vision of a better world yet beyond the present and is some of the most beautiful ever to come out of men's souls or out of that form of expression called Jazz.[46]

This album, recorded at a benefit concert for the short-lived Black Arts Repertory Theatre/School, which Baraka directed, features Coltrane, Ayler, Shepp, trombonist Grachan Moncur, and trumpet player Charles Tolliver.

Many other examples in which jazz was assigned the task of social protest can be cited. In a passage from the liner notes for the album *Extensions* (Blue Note LA006G, 1970), pianist McCoy Tyner summarizes his philosophy of music-making at that time: "Music tells a story — it may summarize the past or redirect the future. Compositions written and played by Black musicians are vehicles to express the struggles and sufferings of Black people."[47] In this instance the listener was also provided with a description of the emotional and pictorial topic of each piece on the album. Tyner, a Black Muslim, also supplied quotations from the Koran, the Moslem book of faith containing the revelations of Mohammed.

Saxophonist John Coltrane produced one of the most poignant examples of program music and protest music in jazz with "Alabama" (*Live at Birdland*, Impulse AS–50, 1963), a haunting modal elegy for the four child victims of a racist's bomb at a church in Birmingham in 1963. The piece presents a sequence of moods: sorrow, resignation, defiance, and hope. This musical prayer is a striking illustration of jazz as a form of "oral history," as the piece immortalizes a particular incident in American history. Details of the music, moreover, were reportedly determined by the speech rhythms of Martin Luther King's eulogy for the slain children.[48] The rhythm of the word "Alabama" (long-long-short-long) can be heard in a phrase that recurs several times as the piece unfolds.

The music of Archie Shepp exhibits many dynamic examples of the union of jazz and contemporary black concerns. Two of his recorded performances, for example, serve as musical memorials to black victims and are labelled as such. Racist violence in the form of a lynching is the theme of a powerful

1964 performance entitled "Rufus (Swung, his face to the wind, then his neck snapped)" on *Four for Trane* (Impulse AS–71, 1964). The following year Shepp responded to the assassination of Malcolm X with the elegy "Malcolm, Malcolm — Semper Malcolm" from the recording *Fire Music* (Impulse AS–86, 1965). According to Nat Hentoff, the composition "is meant to symbolize the various elements in Malcolm's life and spirit, and in the life and spirit of this country's black people." [19] In providing additional commentary on the program of the piece, the artist summarizes the significance of the fallen leader for many American blacks:

> I call it "Malcolm forever" because of my belief in his immortality. I mean he was killed but the significance of what he was will continue and will grow. He was, among other things, the first cat to give actual expression — though he didn't act it out — to much of the hostility most American Negroes feel. I'm not saying that most Negroes want to act it out either, but it's there, and for very good reasons. And a further significance of Malcolm was that toward the end of his life, he was evolving into a sound political realist.
>
> Malcolm knew what it is to be faceless in America and to be sick and tired of that feeling. And he knew the pride of black, that negritude which was bigger than Malcolm himself. There'll be other Malcolms.[50]

With Shepp himself delivering the brief poem as the music commences, the performance becomes part eulogy, part lamentation, and part expression of hope. The music was borrowed from an unfinished work by Shepp intended to pay tribute to another assassinated black leader, Medgar Evers, who was murdered in 1963.

On the same album is found "Los Olvidados" (The Forgotten Ones), which relates to Shepp's work as a counselor and music teacher in Mobilization for Youth, a federally-sponsored program for underprivileged children on the Lower East Side of New York City. Here the message addresses both the good intentions of the saxophonist and the greater struggle to enrich the lives of children in a project that was doomed because of inadequate resources and an ineffectual bureaucracy. The theme of the music, according to Shepp, is "the frustrations of that gig — knowing I couldn't do anything meaningful about that scene."[51]

The name for this work was borrowed from the title of a 1950 Mexican film directed by Luis Buñuel and shown in the United States as *The Young and the Damned.*

Black Nationalist musicians purposefully sought a music that would provide them with an identity that could not be absorbed by the white musical world. They accomplished this in part by being "free." The term not only implied freedom to experiment with new techniques, but more important psychologically, freedom from the musical trappings of Western society — most notably, the popular song, the tempered scale and harmonic system of European music, and the metric strait-jacket of middle-class American popular music.[52] Likewise, the militancy of their social views found a parallel in the rigid meaning they assigned to their music in general. In the words of Archie Shepp, jazz is

> one of the most meaningful social, esthetical contributions to America. . . . It is antiwar; it is opposed to Vietnam; it is for Cuba; it is for the liberation of all people. . . . Why is that so? Because jazz is a music itself born out of oppression, born out of the enslavement of my people.[53]

Because music had been the notable endeavor in which black Americans had been permitted freedom of expression, these black musicians perceived their efforts in this new environment of racial politics as a continuation and a confirmation of that freedom: "Music not only must bring esthetic, but also social order into our lives."[54] In spite of the inflamed pronouncements that accompanied the music of the Black Nationalists, their musical practice was not as exclusive as its proponents would have, perhaps, preferred. Some of their experiments were similar in nature to those conducted by other progressive musicians who acknowledged no association with this socio-religious movement. The fact that Black Nationalists gave their music special meaning or believed that their music communicated their social agenda was a product of the times and its idealism.

Because of its highly experimental nature, its exhausting intensity, and its extra-musical content, the "protest music" of Black Nationalist jazz musicians was rarely able to attract a large portion of the jazz audience. The historical importance of these endeavors, however, must not be minimized by commercial considerations. It is important as well to emphasize that the protest movement in jazz gained currency among black musicians of all ages. Numerous recorded performances by musicians of the preceding generation, most notably drummer Max Roach and bass player Charles Mingus, also exhibit a similar commitment to the black cause and its expression in jazz. In such cases, the musical language often differed from that established by the avant-garde.

Jazz as Religious Expression

Although there has always been a close family relationship among spirituals, gospel music, the blues, and jazz in musical terms, the latter two have evolved and prospered in the realm of secular life. The blues and jazz sprang from the rituals of Friday and Saturday nights; spirituals and gospel soared from the ceremonies of Sunday morning. During the sixties such arbitrary restrictions between sacred and secular were disregarded as leading jazz musicians re-evaluated the role of music in their own lives. Many discovered a vital connection between their spiritual beliefs and their musical activities and deliberately set out to bring these two important aspects of their lives into closer harmony. It is not too far-fetched to propose that some jazz musicians began to perform as preachers, with music taking the place of sermons. Others were content to bear witness to their faith by the nature of their lifestyles and the attitudes reflected in their music. The more noticeable, perhaps, were those who embarked on a spiritual journey into non-Western religious thought and came to perceive their own performances as a form of meditation. In effect, by employing their music to express personal religious convictions, these individuals expanded the jazz tradition in purpose and content.

Jazz and Christianity

In his autobiography, Duke Ellington makes several references to the intersection of his own religious experience and his professional life:

> When I really settled down to read and to think about what
> I was reading in the Bible, I found many things that I had

been feeling all my life without quite understanding them. On becoming more acquainted with the word of the Bible, I began to understand so much more of what I had been taught, and what I thought I had learned about life and about the people in mine.[55]

There have been times when I thought I had a glimpse of God. Sometimes, even when my eyes were closed, I saw. Then when I tried to set my eyes — closed or open — back to the same focus, I had no success, of course. The unprovable fact is that I believe I have had a glimpse of God many times. I believe because believing is believable, and no one can prove it unbelievable.[56]

From these passages it is evident that Christian ideals did not suddenly surface in Ellington the musician during the sixties. It seems more likely that the secular customs of the jazz world had not offered him an opportunity to express his religious convictions in music. That opportunity arose in 1965 when he was invited to perform a concert of sacred music at Grace Cathedral in San Francisco. The jazz master's response to this invitation is memorable: "Now I can say openly what I have been saying to myself on my knees."[57]

Between 1965 and 1973 Duke Ellington created three oratorio-like works for a large complement of performers: *First Sacred Concert* (Grace Cathedral, San Francisco, 1965; excerpts, *A Concert of Sacred Music*, RCA Victor LSP–3582, 1966), *Second Sacred Concert* (Cathedral Church of St. John the Divine, New York City, 1968; Prestige P–24045, n.d.), and *Third Sacred Concert* (Westminster Abbey, London, 1972; RCA SF 8406, 1973). With his band at his side, he presided over performances of this special repertory in many houses of worship of various denominations in the United States and Europe. These pieces have been cited for their grand-scale, multi-movement design in the earlier discussion of structural design (see pages 78–79).

The themes of the "sacred concerts" are Biblical, but the composer's message — his personal feelings about God and religion — is communicated through everyday language with an occasional elegant Ellington turn of phrase and through his music. The first four words of the King James version, "In the beginning God," is the basis of the *First Sacred Concert*. "Praise God," the overriding message of the *Second Sacred Concert,* is translated into an unusual variety of devotional moods and methods, including modern dance and African-American dance. The focus of the *Third Sacred Concert*, which was given its premiere on United Nations Day 1973 (October 24), is international solidarity and peace. The titles of several movements from the *Second Sacred Concert* indicate Ellington's ecumenical testimonial for Christianity: "The Shepherd (Who Watches over the Night Flock)," an instrumental portrait of a Lutheran pastor who ministered to "street people"; "T.G.T.T." (Too Good to Title), music that violates conformity "in the same way that Christ did"; and the vocal solo "Don't Get Down on Your Knees to Pray until You Have Forgiven Everyone."[58] A highlight of the work, the choral finale to the first half titled "It's Freedom," calls for freedom in twenty languages and concludes with what Ellington identifies as "the four freedoms by which I think Billy Strayhorn lived: freedom from hate unconditionally; freedom from self-pity; freedom from fear of doing something that would help someone more than it does him; and freedom from the kind of pride that could make a man feel he was better than his brother."[59]

Ellington's proclamation of Christian ethics through these compositions was widely hailed, but the composer, the Christian witness, remained humble concerning his contributions:

> I think of myself as a messenger boy, one who tries to bring messages to people, not people who have never heard of God, but those who were more or less raised in the guidance of the Church. Now and then we encounter people who say they do not believe. I hate to say that they are out-and-out liars, but I believe they think it is fashionable to speak like that, having been brainwashed by someone beneath them, by someone with a complex who enjoys bringing them to their knees in the worship of the nonexistence of God. They snicker in the dark as they tremble with fright.[60]

His response to those who questioned his motives in writing sacred music reveals his appreciation of how much the jazz musician's role in society had changed during his lifetime: "I have done so not as a matter of career, but in response to a growing understanding of my own vocation. . . ."[61] Significantly enough, Ellington, the creator of more than 2,000 compositions, is known to have considered his "sacred concerts" among his most important works.[62]

Similar in spirit to these non-liturgical and non-sectarian musical extravaganzas by Ellington was the "jazz mass." Thanks to the reforms enacted by the Second Vatican Council at the instigation of Pope John XXIII, the Roman Catholic Church permitted the introduction of vernacular musics into official services. As a result, the jazz mass gained a degree of popularity, especially in urban areas where both an active audience for jazz and an active body of jazz musicians existed. A high percentage of the music created for such services was of a purely utilitarian nature; little was recorded. Two examples of lasting value are Lalo Schifrin's *Jazz Mass* written for flutist Paul Horn, excerpts from which appeared as *Jazz Suite on the Mass Texts* (RCA Victor LPM–3414, 1965), and *Mary Lou's Mass* (1969) by pianist and composer Mary Lou Williams (Mary Records M 102, 1975), a work of great eclecticism that was commissioned by the Vatican.

Jazz and Oriental Religion

According to the African aesthetic of music-making, the musical instrument is considered as a physical extension of the performer; the music then comes through the horn, an expression of the performer's soul. This is the attitude that American jazz musicians have tended to hold. According to the Oriental point of view, by making music, the performer-creator is tapping the cosmos in search of truth and beauty. The sharp contrast here is one of direction. The African is revealing an inner feeling, which goes out from the musician's body. The Oriental is searching for a feeling greater than the individual to bring into the body.

During the sixties many Americans set aside traditional belief systems and investigated various Eastern philosophies and religions. In their search for alternative lifestyles and expression, many jazz artists became strongly influenced by the spiritual and aesthetical aspects of the music of India, which, from the Indian point of view, are its essence. Although the music of India was undoubtedly intellectually stimulating, it was probably its exotic nature and its emotional content — the unremitting cumulative effect of this music — that attracted jazz musicians. Each *rāga*, for example, embodies a definite "ethical" significance and describes a single emotional theme associated with a particular season and hour of the day. It was this attempt to capture a definite ethical or emotional meaning in music that fascinated a number of prominent jazz artists. Jazz in this context became a socio-religious philosophy in action. In his short discussion of the significance of Oriental attitudes to black jazz musicians, Sidran emphasizes the social factor:

> Eastern philosophies are spiritual postures with direct secular application, the kind of secular spirituality toward which black culture had been moving, through music, for years. Further, Oriental religions endow their gods with *human* faculties, which may have appealed to the American Negroes' demand for justice in the *here* and *now*. Finally, Eastern philosophies are centered on absolute *resistence*, like the existential *no*, to the currents of world affairs. As Stokely Carmichael stressed, the black man's first problem was getting over the fear of saying *no* to white value structures. The appeal of Indian music was based also on its role in society: it is neither "Art" music in the Western sense nor "popular" music but, rather, "exalted folk" music.[63]

The attraction of Oriental ideas was not limited to blacks, as a number of white jazz musicians adopted a similar spiritual and musical posture. Flutist Paul Horn was among the early prominent converts. Shortly after his first serious exposure to Indian music in 1965, he became a disciple of the well-known Indian spiritual leader, the Maharishi Mahesh Yogi. Horn learned his mentor's system of meditation in India on the banks of the Ganges and returned to the United States as one of the first twelve teachers of Transcendental Meditation in this country.[64] His musical endeavors, notably his improvising within the musical and ethical frame of the *rāga*, have already been described (see pages 52–53), but it is useful to cite the programmatic content of representative performances on his albums *Paul Horn in India* (World Pacific WPS 21447) and *Paul Horn in Kashmir* (World Pacific WP–1445), reissued as *Paul Horn in India* (Blue Note, LA529–H2, 1975): "Raga Desh" depicts a melancholy mood in the evening; "Manj-Khamaj" describes "a playful situation between Radha and Krishna"; and "Raga Kerwan" is an expression of praise of beauty and nature for the hours between 9:00 P.M. and midnight.[65]

Guitarist John McLaughlin and pianist and harpist Alice Coltrane stand out as additional exponents of associating jazz with Oriental spiritualism. Their insistence that their music is a function of their beliefs is emphasized by the presence of published explanations of their feelings and purposes, often as the annotations to recordings. McLaughlin, a leader in the movement to fuse jazz and rock toward the end of the decade, was given the holy name "Mahavishnu" by his guru, Sri Chinmoy. The guitarist in turn gave this name to the ensemble he formed, the Mahavishnu Orchestra. The following statement by McLaughlin suggests the single-minded devotion of the convert:

> My music is an offering to the supreme being. Through the grace of Sri Chinmoy I've become more aware of the presence of God and this awareness is manifesting itself in multiple ways. God is the supreme musician, the soul of music and the spirit of music. I'm trying to reach him by allowing myself to become his instrument; that's all I want to become in all aspects of life.[66]

Alice Coltrane provided a similar testimonial in the title and notes for her album *Journey in Satchidananda* (Impulse AS–9203, 1970), which features saxophonist Pharoah Sanders and makes use of the harp and non-Western instruments. The name of her spiritual mentor is Satchidananda, whom she names as a dynamic resource in her personal life:

> Direct inspiration for JOURNEY IN SATCHIDANANDA comes from my meeting and association with someone who is near and dear to me. I am speaking of my own beloved spiritual perceptor, Swami Satchidananda. Swamiji is the first example I have seen in recent years of Universal Love or God in action. He expresses an impersonal love, which encompasses thousands of people. Anyone listening to this selection should try to envision himself floating on an ocean of Satchidanandiji's love, which is literally carrying countless devotees across the vicissitudes and stormy blasts of life to the other shore. Satchidananda means knowledge, existence, bliss.[67]

Another notable performance in this collection concerns the Hindu deity Shiva. In appropriate fashion, the artist concludes her remarks to listeners in the liner notes with a benediction: "I hope that this album will be a form of meditation and a spiritual awakening for those who listen with their inner ear. Om shanti."[68]

The Black Avant-Garde and Spiritualism

A parallel development to the self-acknowledged investigations of Oriental religious practices by jazz musicians was the appearance of a less easily definable spiritual movement among members of the black avant-garde. Baraka has stressed this religious motivation in the playing of prominent figures:

> The new music began by calling itself "free," and this is social and is in direct commentary on the scene it appears in. Once free, it is spiritual. . . .
> The new jazz people never had that practical God, as practical, and seek the mystical God both emotionally and intellectually.
> John Coltrane, Albert Ayler, Sun-Ra, Pharoah Sanders come to mind immediately as God seekers.[69]

In the last years of his life, John Coltrane sought to combine his music with a new-found spiritual awareness dating from a religious experience in 1957. His first effort in this regard, the recording *A Love Supreme* (Impulse S–77, 1964), includes as accessories to the instrumental performances programmatic titles indicating religious content, chanting by members of the ensemble, and a written testimonial in the form of a sacred poem by Coltrane himself. A highly personal letter from the artist to his listeners (printed on the album jacket) documents his intentions:

> DEAR LISTENER:
> ALL PRAISE BE TO GOD TO WHOM ALL PRAISE IS DUE.
> Let us pursue Him in the righteous path. Yes it is true: "seek and ye shall find." Only through Him can we know the most wondrous bestowal.
> During the year 1957, I experienced, by the grace of God, a spiritual awakening which was to lead me to a richer, fuller, more productive life. At that time, in gratitude, I humbly asked to be given the means and privilege to make others happy through music. I feel this has been granted through His grace. ALL PRAISE TO GOD.

As time and events moved on, a period of irresolution did prevail. I entered into a phase which was contradictory to the pledge and away from the esteemed path; but thankfully, now and again through the unerring and merciful hand of God, I do perceive and have been duly re-informed of His OMNIPOTENCE, and of our need for, and dependence on Him. At this time I would like to tell you that NO MATTER WHAT ... IT IS WITH GOD. HE IS GRACIOUS AND MERCIFUL. HIS WAY IS THROUGH LOVE, IN WHICH WE ALL ARE. IT IS TRULY — A LOVE SUPREME —

This album is a humble offering to Him. An attempt to say "THANK YOU GOD" through our work, even as we do in our hearts and with our tongues. May He help and strengthen all men in every good endeavor.[70]

The fervency and sincerity of this public confession are intensified in a religious poem — a prayer — that Coltrane has written and made public with the recorded performance.

I will do all I can to be worthy of Thee O Lord.
It all has to do with it.
Thank you God.
Peace.
There is none other.
God is. It is so beautiful.
Thank you God. God is all.
Help us to resolve our fears and weaknesses.
Thank you God.
In You all things are possible.
We know God made us so.
Keep your eye on God.
God is. He always was. He always will be.
No matter what . . . It is God.
He is gracious and merciful.
It is most important that I know Thee.
Words, sounds, speech, men, memory, thoughts, fears
    and emotions — time — all related . . . all made from
    one . . . all make in one.
Blessed be His name.
Thought waves — heat waves — all vibrations — all
    paths lead to God. Thank you God.
His way . . . it is so lovely . . . it is gracious.
It is merciful — Thank you God.
One thought can produce millions of vibrations
    and they all go back to God . . . everything does.
Thank you God.

Have no fear . . . believe . . . Thank you God.
The universe has many wonders. God is all.
His way . . . it is so wonderful.
Thoughts — deeds — vibrations, etc.
They all go back to God and He cleanses all.
He is gracious and merciful . . . Thank you God.

Glory to God . . . God is so alive.
God is.
God loves.
May I be acceptable in Thy sight.
We are all one in His grace.
The fact that we do exist is acknowledgement of Thee
   O Lord.
Thank you God.
God will wash away all our tears . . . He always has . . .
He always will.
Seek Him every day, in all ways seek God everday.
Let us sing all songs to God.
To whom all praise is due . . . praise God.
No road is an easy one but they all go back to God.
With all we share God.
It is all with God.
It is all with Thee.
Obey the Lord.
Blessed is He.
We are all from one thing . . . the will of God . . .
   Thank you God.
I have seen God — I have seen ungodly — none can be
   greater — none can compare to God.
Thank you God.
He will remake us . . . He always has and He always will.
It is true — blessed be His name — Thank you God.
God breathes through us so completely . . . so gently we
   hardly feel it . . . yet, it is our everything.
Thank you God
ELATION — ELEGANCE — EXALTATION —
All from God.
Thank you God. Amen.[71]

There were no precedents in the history of jazz for this public display of highly personal religious sentiments. In the context of the times, however, such extraordinary behavior received widespread approval.

Although Coltrane's prayer reflects the rhetorical style of many black preachers (both of his grandfathers were Protestant

ministers), it seems clear that the "God" to whom the saxophonist offers praise is not the emotionally fraught fundamentalist
God of many American blacks. Such verses as

> Words, sound speech, men, memory, thoughts,
> Fears and emotions — time — all related . . .
> All made from one . . . all made in one.[72]

strongly suggest the unity of all aspects of existence characteristic of non-Western religions. Coltrane, however, was not primarily interested in espousing a particular Oriental, Middle
Eastern, or African philosophy. He was searching for a universal
concept uniting all faiths.[73] The catalyst for his 1957 "spiritual awakening" was his introduction to the tenets of Islam by
his wife Naima and their re-enforcement by his pianist McCoy
Tyner. In his search for enlightenment, Coltrane devoted considerable time to reading books on religion and philosophical
thought, such as *Autobiography of a Yogi* by Paramhansa Yoga-
nanda; *Commentaries on Living* by Jiddu Krishnamurti; the works
of Plato, Aristotle, the American spiritualist Edgar Cayce, and
Kahil Gibran; and books about egyptology and scientology.[74] He
also enjoyed an extended correspondence concerning the nature of Indian music with Ravi Shankar, which resulted in the
meeting of the two famous musicians. (Coltrane named a son
after the Indian musician.)

One commentator has reported that specific details of *A Love
Supreme* are based on a system of occult numerical symbolism that
Coltrane learned from his reading of the *cabala* (also *kabbalah*),
books of Jewish mysticism dating from the Middle Ages:

> By the numbers, then; if you listen carefully to the con-
> tinuous chanting of "a love supreme" that separates the first
> and second sections of the composition, you can count the
> repetition of this phrase nineteen times.
> Separate that number; one means alone; nine stands for
> universal. One creative man alone, either with or against
> the universe, but definitely of the universal consciousness.
> One plus nine equals ten. And, according to the Kabbala,
> there are ten manifestations of God.[75]

Once again, it is fair to note that not only is this a rather remarkable association for jazz, but also the compositional methods are

equally novel in this sphere. As a result, Coltrane joins such illustrious fine-art composers as J. S. Bach and Mozart in using numerology for a higher compositional purpose.

As an ecumenical prayer for peace, *A Love Supreme* is organized as four progressive phases in spiritual self-awareness: "Acknowledgement," "Resolution," "Pursuance," and "Psalm (A Love Supreme)." In his annotations, Len Lyons speculates on Coltrane's careful regard for the extra-musical aspects of the performance:

> A Love Supreme takes as a premise the Indian notion that scales and sounds can be used to convey specific emotional meanings. The gong, for example, generally signifies an exalted presence, the "One" to whom Coltrane addresses this music. The free-time opening of "Acknowledgement" and the closing of "Psalm" symbolize the transition into and out of the devotional state. The instrument's "screams" are ecstatic releases. The clear, strong middle-register "call" is the energetic offering of the music itself. That Coltrane had these particular meanings in mind is, of course, conjecture. The point is that his musical "cues" achieve these effects throughout, evoking more predictable and deeper responses in the listener because of their consistency.[76]

It has been reported that Coltrane and his sidemen performed this music at least once, in 1965, in a church setting in Brooklyn; Coltrane recited his poem before the music was presented.[77]

In discussing a later recording with a title implying similar intentions, *Meditations* (Impulse AS–9110, 1966), Coltrane commented directly on the relationship between his music and his idealism:

> Once you become aware of this force for unity in life, you can't forget it. It becomes part of everything you do. In that respect, this is an extension of A Love Supreme since my conception of that force keeps changing shape. My goal in meditating on this through music, however, remains the same. And that is to uplift people, as much as I can. To inspire them to realize more and more of their capabilities for living meaningful lives.[78]

The famous saxophonist continued these spiritual explorations in the few remaining years of his life.

The example offered by John Coltrane was of great influence both musically and spiritually. Before his death, the younger generation of radical black jazz musicians had elevated him to the position of elder statesman and cult hero.[79] Further testimony to this aspect of his contribution can be found in his posthumous reputation. In *The Making of Jazz*, James Lincoln Collier gives his thoughtful essay about Coltrane the subtext "Jazz Messiah" and in his introduction makes the following remarkable declaration: "John Coltrane, in sum, was seen — and still is by many — not merely as a great jazz musician, but as a spiritual leader on a level with the founders of the world's great religions."[80]

The music of saxophonist Albert Ayler evokes a religious experience much better known to American blacks. The titles of his pieces and his albums recall the imagery of traditional black religion in America. Such words as "spirits," "ghosts," and "angels" reappear in titles, and his music — although highly personal and difficult to understand — exhibits an affinity with the music of fundamentalist black churches in its unrestrained emotional content as well as the hymn tunes and spiritual march music. The recordings *Spirits* (Transatlantic 130, 1964), *Ghosts* (Fontana 925 888 ZY, 1964), and *Spirits Rejoice* (ESP 1020, 1965) exemplify Ayler's religious concerns.

Perhaps the most idiosyncratic example of spiritualism and mysticism in jazz at any point in its history is found in the work of Sun Ra, whose extreme individualism has caused his considerable talents and achievements to go unappreciated by the general jazz public. The decidedly eccentric Ra has concerned himself with "the evolution of cosmic consciousness" by exploring inner and outer space through music and poetry. The extramusical trappings for his musical performances are heterogeneous and highly theatrical in nature. His philosophy, while never truly summarized or clearly stated, is related in his own highly personal manner to perceptions concerning, among other topics, the culture of ancient Egypt and to an open-ended "space-age" mysticism.

Space-age imagery in the titles of works, in the extravagant staging of his theatrical performances, and in other aspects of public relations can be found throughout Sun Ra's work. He made his first recording under his assumed name, Sun Ra, in 1956. Before that time, he had been known as Le Sony'r Ra, apparently an affectation of his nickname "Sonny." His large jazz ensemble of dedicated disciples has been publicly identified as the "Arkestra" (obviously related to "orchestra") since that time, with changing qualifications that include the "Myth-Science Arkestra," the "Solar Arkestra," the "Astro-Infinity Arkestra," and the "Intergalactic-Research Arkestra." Likewise, the programmatic titles of his compositions and the language of his poetry are distinctive because of references indicating his contention that his music is a function of his unorthodox belief system: astro, heliocentric, cosmic, galactic, planetary.

Performances by Sun Ra, at least by 1967, began to take on the appearance of private religious rites. Many performances took place under non-commercial circumstances, unannounced to the general public, but at the same time known to a small group of devoted followers. Sun Ra and his musicians performed in glittering costumes of flowing "Saturn gowns," "galaxy caps," and "cosmic rosaries." Lighting was contrived to provide sensational visual effects at appropriate moments; flashing lights were attached to the headdresses of musicians and dancers. The musicians often followed their leader in a kind of "snake dance" through the audience, playing, chanting, and flashing their lights. The musicians also periodically and conspicuously gazed into the distance as if looking for answers in the heavens. "Occasionally, the culmination of a Sun Ra show involves a telescope which the master sets up next to his organ, and through which he searches for his 'home planet Saturn' during special 'cosmic climaxes.'"[81] This ritual in performance continues up to the present day. The favorite chant of Sun Ra and his musicians is, "Space is the place!"

In a 1970 interview, Sun Ra assessed his music:

> I'm not playing Space Music as the ultimate reach anymore. That is, not in the interplanetary sense alone. I'm playing intergalactic music, which is beyond the other idea of space music, because it is of the natural infinity of the eternal universe. . . . The intergalactic music in its present phase of presentation will be correlative to the key synopsis of the past and to the uncharted multi-potential places outside the bounds of the limited earth-eternity future. The intergalactic music is in hieroglyphic sound: an abstract analysis and synthesis of man's relationship to the universe, visible and invisible first man and second man.[82]

Whatever the meaning of this cryptic passage, these remarks do serve a sample of the novelty of Sun Ra's message and his rhetoric in the context of jazz — and the extra-musical content as understood by its creator.

The distinctive nature of Sun Ra's personal vision has elicited interesting comments by observers. Baraka has stressed both its novelty and its spiritual character:

> Sun-Ra is spiritually oriented. He understands "the future" as an ever widening comprehension of what space is. . . . It is science-fact that Sun-Ra is interested in, not science-fiction. . . . So the future revealed is man explained to himself. . . .
> Sun-Ra's is a new content for jazz, for Black music, but it's merely, again the spiritual defining itself.[83]

Indeed, there can be little doubt that, in actual detail of this worldview and its resulting ritual, Sun Ra's music represented new content for jazz as Baraka pointed out. An appreciation for the historical perspective of African-American music, as expressed by Ekkehard Jost, however, reveals that the concept of such a presentation is not as new as it seems:

> The roots of this show lie rather in the origins of Afro-American music: in the rites of the voodoo cult, a blend of magic, music and dance; and in the vaudeville shows of itinerant troupes of actors and musicians, where there was room for gaudily tinselled costumes and the stunts of supple acrobats, as well as the emotional depths of blues sung by a Ma Rainey or a Bessie Smith.[84]

The music in Sun Ra's repertory is another indicator of the strong jazz tradition. His musical idiom is a fascinating synthesis of many of the musical liberties of the sixties with obvious references to the earlier styles of swing and bop.

CONCLUSION

At the same time that jazz musicians were vigorously exploring the technical nature of their music, many among them were also finding new purposes and new meanings for their efforts. By the end of the sixties jazz had appeared in various guises: as history lessons and travelogues, as tonal paintings and psychological odysseys, as social protest and propaganda, as public worship and private meditation. A number of such pieces are among the most characteristic of the times and appear to be among the finest examples of jazz of the era. Especially memorable are the white-hot convictions with which the musicians presented their music and the faithfulness of their endeavors to the currents and countercurrents of the sixties. With the waning of interest or passing from focus of that decade's particular artistic and social crusades, the motivation for the continuation of some of these practices diminished. Many would argue, however, that these conditions have not been satisfactorily addressed and will return to importance. What seems most significant in a larger sense is the setting of precedent. Since the sixties, jazz artists have been able to participate in a remarkably broad tradition.

---

1   Frank Kofsky, *Black Nationalism and the Revolution in Music* (New York: Pathfinder Press, 1970), pp. 46–49.

2   *Ibid.*, 46.

3   Jennifer Jordan reports that this special responsibility was also assumed by young black writers at this time. See Jennifer Jordan, "Cultural Nationalism in the 1960s: Politics and Poetry," *Race, Politics, and Culture: Critical Essays on the Radicalism of the 1960s*, ed. Adolph Reed, Jr. (Westport, Ct.: Greenwood Press, 1986), pp. 29–60.

4   Dominique-René de Lerma, record liner notes to *Afro-American Symphony* by William Grant Still et al. (Columbia M 32782, 1974).

5   Sonny Rollins, record liner notes to *Freedom Suite* by Sonny Rollins (Riverside OJC–067/RLP–258, 1958).

6   Orrin Keepnews, record liner notes to *Freedom Suite* by Sonny Rollins (Riverside OJC–067/RLP–258, 1958).

7   *Ibid.*

8   Kofsky, *Black Nationalism and the Revolution in Music*, pp. 50–51.

9   Oliver Nelson, record liner notes to *Afro/American Sketches* by Oliver Nelson (Prestige 7225, 1961).

10   See Stanley Dance, record liner notes to *New Orleans Suite* by Duke Ellington (Atlantic SD–1580, 1971).

11   Braud, who spent his early years in New Orleans, was a member of the Ellington band between 1926 and 1935; Bechet, who spent much of his career abroad, was a member of the Ellington band briefly before his move to Europe; and Jackson, a native of New Orleans, joined with Ellington in 1958 for performances of his *Black and Tan Fantasy*.

12   Neil Tesser, record liner notes to *The Far East Suite* by Duke Ellington (LPM/LSP–3782, 1966; reissued Bluebird 7640–1–RB, 1988).

13   Edward Kennedy Ellington, *Music Is My Mistress* (Garden City, N.Y.: Doubleday, 1973; reprinted New York: Da Capo, 1976), pp. 301–30.

14   Herbie Hancock, record liner notes to *Maiden Voyage* by Herbie Hancock (Blue Note BLP–84195, 1965).

15 Nora Kelly, record liner notes to *Maiden Voyage* by Herbie Hancock (Blue Note BLP–84195, 1965).

16 Wayne Shorter, quoted in Leonard Feather, record liner notes to *Odyssey of Iska* by Wayne Shorter (Blue Note 84363, 1970).

17 *Ibid.*

18 Wayne Shorter, "Odyssey of Iska," record liner notes to *Odyssey of Iska* by Wayne Shorter (Blue Note 84363, 1970).

19 Dave Brubeck, record liner notes to *Jazz Impressions of Japan* by the Dave Brubeck Quartet (Columbia PC 9012, 1964).

20 *Ibid.* The translations of the Haiku poetry have been taken from *Little Pictures of Japan* (Chicago: The Book House for Children, 1925), edited by Olive Beaupre Miller, and *An Introduction to Haiku* (Garden City, N.Y.: Doubleday, 1958) by Harold G. Henderson. Such Haiku masters as Basho, Issa, and Buson are represented.

21 L. T. Beauchamp [Chicago Beau], record liner notes to *The Lowlands* by Archie Shepp and Philly Joe Jones (Fantasy 86018, 1969).

22 *Ibid.*

23 *Ibid.*

24 Julio Finn, record liner notes to *The Lowlands* by Archie Shepp and Philly Joe Jones (Fantasy 86018, 1969).

25 Augustus Arnold, record liner notes to *The Lowlands* by Archie Shepp and Philly Joe Jones (Fantasy 86018, 1969).

26 See Adolph Reed, Jr., ed., *Race, Politics, and Culture: Critical Essays on the Radicalism of the 1960s* (Westport, Ct.: Greenwood Press, 1986).

27 See Imamu Amiri Baraka (LeRoi Jones), "The Phenomenon of *Soul* in African-American Music," *The Music: Reflections on Jazz and Blues* (New York: William Morrow, 1987), pp. 268–76.

28 For example, in music, the important scholarly journal *The Black Perspective in Music* began publication.

29 Imamu Amiri Baraka (LeRoi Jones), *Blues People* (New York: William Morrow, 1963), p. 218.

30 For additional information on the beliefs and activities of the Nation of Islam, see C. Eric Lincoln, *The Black Muslims in America* (Boston: Beacon, 1961).

31 See Malcolm X and Alex Haley, *The Autobiography of Malcolm X* (New York: Ballantine, 1964), and *Malcolm X Speaks*, ed. George Bretiman (New York: Grove, 1965).

32 Malcolm X and Haley, *The Autobiography of Malcolm X*, pp. 395–96.

33 See the essay "Black Revolution and Black Music: The Career of Malcolm X" in Kofsky, *Black Nationalism and the Revolution in Music*, pp. 249–62.

34 Dave Helland, "Greg Osby: Open on All Sides," *down beat* 56 (October 1989), 26.

35 Kimberly W. Benston, "Introduction," *Imamu Amiri Baraka (LeRoi Jones): A Collection of Critical Essays* (Englewood Cliffs, N.J.: Prentice-Hall, 1978), p. 3.

36 Imamu Amiri Baraka (LeRoi Jones), *The Autobiography of LeRoi Jones* (New York: Freundlich Books, 1984), p. 267.

37   Lloyd W. Brown, *Amiri Baraka* (Boston: Twayne, 1980), p. 53. This author summarizes and assesses Baraka's music criticism as part of a study of all his writings (pp. 47–58). There are also several studies of Baraka's music criticism in Benston, *Imamu Amiri Baraka*.

38   A collection of Baraka's important writings on this subject, many conceived originally as liner notes, are published in *Black Music* (New York: William Morrow, 1967); this volume also includes his defiant essay "Jazz and the White Critic" from 1963.

39   Interestingly enough, *The Jazz Scene* by the British writer Francis Newton (London: MacGibbon & Kee, 1959) contains a curious essay entitled "Jazz as a Protest" (pp. 260–77). The author's arguments concentrate on the social perceptions of jazz as a "vulgar" and rebellious music caused by its lower-class and black associations rather than on any purposeful efforts by musicians. In doing so, the essay tends to place the jazz protests of the sixties in even greater relief.

40   See David Evans, "Black American Music as a Symbol of Identity," *Jazzforschung* 13 (1981), 105–16.

41   Imamu Amiri Baraka (LeRoi Jones), *Blues People*, 130–31.

42   Archie Shepp, "An Artist Speaks Bluntly," *down beat* 32 (December 16, 1965), 11.

43   Gus Matzorkis, "Down Where We Live: Today's Avant-Garde Revolution as Seen in Light of Jazz' Long History of Internal Strife 1," *down beat* 33 (April 7, 1966), 21.

44   Archie Shepp, quoted without documentation in Kofsky, *Black Nationalism and the Revolution in Music*, p. 9.

45   Imamu Amiri Baraka (LeRoi Jones), *Black Music* (New York: William Morrow, 1967), p. 209.

46   Steve Young, record liner notes to *The New Wave in Jazz* by various artists (Impulse AS–90, 1965).

47   McCoy Tyner, record liner notes to *Extensions* by McCoy Tyner (Blue Note LA006G, 1970).

48   Len Lyons, *The 101 Best Jazz Albums: A History of Jazz on Records* (New York: William Morrow, 1980), p. 285.

49   Nat Hentoff, record liner notes to *Fire Music* by Archie Shepp (Impulse AS–86, 1965).

50   Archie Shepp, quoted in *ibid.*

51   *Ibid.*

52   Baraka, *Black Music*, p. 209.

53   Quoted without documentation in Kofsky, *Black Nationalism and the Revolution in Music*, pp. 140–41.

54   Archie Shepp, record liner notes to *Live at the Donaueschingen Festival* by Archie Shepp (BASF–20651, 1972).

55   Ellington, *Music Is My Mistress*, p. 259.

56   *Ibid.*, 260.

57   *Ibid.*, 261.

58   *Ibid.*, 270–79. The outline of the program of the *Second Sacred Concert* is given here, complete with commentary by Ellington.

59   *Ibid.*, 275. Billy Strayhorn (1915–1967), composer, arranger, and

pianist, was a longtime friend and collaborator with Ellington.
60   *Ibid.*, 267–68.
61   Edward Kennedy Ellington, record liner notes to *Second Sacred Concert* by Duke Ellington (Prestige 24045).
62   Stanley Dance, record liner notes to *Third Sacred Concert: The Majesty of God* by Duke Ellington (RCA SF 8406, 1973).
63   Ben Sidran, *Black Talk* (New York: Holt, Rinehart & Winston, 1971), p. 141.
64   Robert Palmer, record liner notes to *Paul Horn in India* by Paul Horn and native Indian instrumentalists (Blue Note LA529–H2, reissued 1975).
65   *Ibid.*
66   Quoted without documentation in Irwin Stambler, *Encyclopedia of Pop, Rock & Soul* (New York: St. Martin's Press, 1974), p. 322.
67   Alice Coltrane, record liner notes to *Journey in Satchidananda* by Alice Coltrane (Impulse AS–9203, 1970).
68   *Ibid.*
69   Baraka, *Black Music*, p. 193.
70   John Coltrane, "A Love Supreme," record liner notes to *A Love Supreme* by John Coltrane (Impulse S–77, 1964).
71   *Ibid.*
72   *Ibid.*
73   Pauline Rivelli, "Alice Coltrane Interview," *Black Giants*, ed. Pauline Rivelli and Robert Levin (New York: World Publishing, 1970), p. 123.
74   J. C. Thomas, *Chasin' the Trane: The Music and Mystique of John Coltrane* (Garden City, N.Y.: Doubleday, 1975; reprinted New York: Da Capo, 1976), p. 118.
75   *Ibid.*, 185.
76   Lyons, *The 101 Best Jazz Albums*, p. 285.
77   Thomas, *Chasin' the Trane*, pp. 193–94.
78   Quoted without documentation in Nat Hentoff, record liner notes to *Meditations* by John Coltrane (Impulse AS–9110, 1966).
79   See Thomas, *Chasin' the Trane*. This text is filled with hundreds of testimonials by jazz musicians as well as other individuals describing the influence of Coltrane.
80   James Lincoln Collier, *The Making of Jazz: A Comprehensive History* (Boston: Houghton Mifflin, 1978), p. 478.
81   Joachim-Ernst Berendt, *The Jazz Book*, trans. by Dan Morgenstern, Helmut Bredigkeit, and Barbara Bredigkeit (New York: Lawrence Hill, 1975), p. 359.
82   Sun Ra, quoted in Tam Fiofori, "Sun Ra's Space Odyssea," *down beat* 37 (May 14, 1970), 16.
83   Baraka, *Black Music*, pp. 198–99.
84   Ekkehard Jost, *Free Jazz* (Graz: Universal, 1974), p. 191.

The Legacy of the Sixties
and a Perspective

THE LEGACY

The decade of the sixties was like no other in the history of jazz:
the mighty river that had represented the mainstream of the jazz
tradition up to that time was diverted into countless streams.
Some of these spilled wildly across the floodplains; some were
strengthened by contact with other bodies of water; others me-
andered; others dried up. The musicians themselves, acting as
an army of self-indulgent engineers, forced the river beyond its
banks according to their own individual interests. The original
current, much reduced, continued to flow. By any standard,
however, much ground was under water! Some of these developments might have been predicted on musical terms; several of
them had been initiated in the late fifties. Others appear to have
been timely responses to the distinctive cultural profile of the
sixties.

 The musical results were dramatic. The general uniformity
of style characteristic of earlier periods in the history of jazz
no longer existed. The tradition of jazz performance as inherited from earlier decades continued, but alongside it flourished
the fundamental re-evaluation of the methods by which that
music was produced. This circumstance resulted in the creation
of styles of jazz in which once-uncontested procedures or conventions were replaced by new systems of order. Radical approaches, which included the abandonment of the metrical conditions favorable for swing (the concept), of the popular song as
a basis for improvisation, and of the distribution of labor within
the jazz ensemble, required reformers to make basic musical
choices — a category of decisions never before confronted by
their predecessors. Each of the elements of music — melody,
harmony, meter, rhythm, form, timbre — was investigated for

new expressive potential. The efforts of one musician or group of musicians differed drastically from the jazz created by peers.

Simultaneously, the mainstream was also being reworked as a result of the diffusion of musical interests held by jazz musicians. Those interests ranged from a fascination for the musics of non-Western cultures to a concern for the techniques and aesthetics of the fine-art avant-garde, from an attraction to recent developments in popular music to the logical extension of jazz resources. The diversity of resources introduced into the music-making process and the variety of purposes assigned by the players to their music reflected the breadth of these interests.

The most superficial, yet far-reaching, manifestation of this spirit of experimentation appeared in the introduction of new instruments to jazz performance. Of enduring importance was the widespread acceptance of the fruits of recent technology in the form of electronic instruments. The expansion of the timbral palette of jazz was accompanied by an emphasis on sound itself. Jazz compositions and improvisations conceived as vehicles for the embellishment or development of theme coexisted with jazz compositions and improvisations conceived as explorations of pure sound. With the influence of rock and roll near the end of the decade came dynamic increases in volume, and like many rock musicians, many jazz artists — fortified with the incredible sonic capabilities provided by modern technology — were unable to resist bombarding listeners with amplified sound.

The reasons for this explosion of intense creativity in jazz, which might be likened by an optimist to an identity crisis and by a pessimist to a nervous breakdown, are both musical and social. Jazz had thrived for approximately sixty years, and the music had grown substantially within a framework of performance practice conventions. Many musicians, in effect, adopted the attitude that the framework had been used up, that it had become a straitjacket or at least an impediment to fresh and timely solutions to jazz-making, and that for the music to go forward, the framework had to be altered or even discarded. This musical dilemma occurred at the same time that American culture experienced its own social catharsis. Idealists and activists questioned almost every commonplace in the fabric of American life and demanded, often with force and sometimes with naïveté, new

solutions to age-old problems. The polarization of the establishment and the counter-culture, galvanized by the civil rights
movement and the war in Vietnam, became a fact of life. These
developments made for provocative times for artists of all kinds.
Jazz musicians were confronted with special challenges and op-
portunities because of the confluence of national social unrest
and their own musical quandary.

Thus, the sixties became a period of experimentation and
enrichment in jazz history. It is evident that many of the particular avenues for investigation, however interesting or controversial, were only temporary phenomena or catalysts for further refinement. Metric-tonal jazz did indeed survive the tempest, but
not without modifications and a respect for new possibilities.
Furthermore, these efforts were not examples of capricious or
eccentric behavior. Jazz musicians sincerely attempted to communicate in terms of their environment. The social and political
milieu of the sixties exerted a powerful influence over these men
and women. Their music dramatically mirrored the activism of
the decade and the search for alternatives to patterns of behavior and traditional ideals. It is noteworthy that the term "jazz,"
more than ever before, fell into disfavor as a generic catchword
to identify successfully the widely divergent styles of music produced by jazz musicians. The musicians themselves were most
critical of the use of the term.

A PERSPECTIVE

In retrospect, it appears that the sixties served as a watershed in the history of jazz in several important respects. There is
enough evidence to propose that the musical experiences of that
decade have marked off jazz history into two rather distinctive
phases or practices. The earlier of these may be described as
focused, conventional, progressive, and even somewhat restrictive. The more recent may be characterized as expansive, toler-
ant, static. In his survey of jazz history, Max Harrison described
many of the developments in jazz after 1960 under the rubric
"Freedom and Exoticism."[1] In effect, he is suggesting a comparison of a similar kind.

Before the sixties it is possible to identify a continuous line of evolution in the jazz style and in the jazz language. There was always a rich array of particular dialects, but the family relationships were rarely obscure. By concentrating on musicians whose ideas are the most progressive, moreover, historians have tended to make the notion of uniformity of style more narrow than actual practice, but the fact remains that the majority of jazz musicians in each generation shared a common language. Nor does the awareness that older styles of jazz did not miraculously disappear once they had been superseded by new developments weaken this observation.

By comparison, the sixties offered an astonishing number of contrasting jazz styles. This, of course, was the result of the grand-scale experimentation generated by the times and an emphasis on individual expression that differed greatly from earlier jazz practices. The wholesale re-evaluation of the conventions of jazz-making and its purpose as well as the intoxicating promise of new musical ideas from the Third World left a legacy of music by jazz musicians of such diversity that the differences often seem much greater that similarities.

In 1970 Leonard Feather acknowledged this trend in liner notes for the album *Odyssey of Iska* by saxophonist Wayne Shorter:

> One uses the word jazz reluctantly in times like these, for clearly the idiom as we have known it, once a central rhythmic and harmonic facet of Shorter's identity, now has become one of many elements that have reached far beyond the purlieus of any one pigeonholed music. To put it in more basic terms, jazz is no longer his sole bag; it is rather one of many tools in a larger and more capacious bag that is cosmic in scope.[2]

The fusion phenomenon that underscored so many of the experiments of the sixties and the resulting creation of musical "hybrids" caused one commentator, John L. Fell, to call into question a future for jazz: "Jazz is so shifting into mixtures with other forms that it is unlikely to survive as an autonomous form."[3] In subsequent years this plurality of styles, nevertheless, appears to have become the status quo. Writing a decade later than Feather, Max Harrison declared that

> jazz no longer has a *lingua franca*. There is instead an extreme diversity of styles and methods, and this situation is

international. Like classical music and the other arts, most notably painting, jazz has entered a post-modernist phase: all styles, the music of all periods, are, it seems, valid.

Jazz musicians continue to speak with many voices. Since the sixties there has existed a broad spectrum of musical styles, bridging performances that might be labelled conservative and even old-fashioned and performances that exhibit a sense of stylistic adventure.

In addition, since the sixties the weight of history has made a considerable impact. The great interest in the history of jazz by music scholars, both in Europe and America, has produced an ever-growing body of valuable musicological literature on the subject and has tended to "legitimize" the place of jazz as a worthwhile endeavor and a meaningful subject for study in the university setting. The benefit of this development to younger jazz artists — contributing to the creation of a broader audience of educated consumers who have cultivated an appreciation of the accomplishments of jazz musicians — is, nonetheless, indirect. It might be argued that those who profit the most are those holding the copyrights to the enduring recordings of yesteryear and older musicians whose performances maintain a link with the illustrious past.

Young musicians have demonstrated their awareness of the history of jazz in their performances. It has always been true, jazz being a product of a kind of oral tradition, that each successive generation of jazz musicians propels itself forward from the musical language of its preceding generation. Yet, in rather uncharacteristic fashion, many contemporary jazz musicians seem to have reached back further in time for inspiration. The achievements of Charlie Parker and Dizzy Gillespie, and, to an even greater degree, of Miles Davis, John Coltrane, and Ornette Coleman have been echoed for several decades now.

This phenomenon represents another bit of evidence that the sixties constitute a watershed in the history of jazz. Since then, there has been no commanding leader to rally jazz musicians — no beacon to lead the way into the future — no masterful innovator to bend the course of jazz in one direction — in the manner of Louis Armstrong, Charlie Parker, Miles Davis, John Coltrane, and Ornette Coleman. This fact, perhaps, accounts for the recycling of ideas and self-consciousness heard in so much of the music. There seems to have been no "new beginnings" of the depth and scope of Coleman's free jazz and the modal playing of Davis and Coltrane since the years of ferment surrounding 1960.[5]

Before the sixties, moreover, the rhythmic content of jazz in all styles was closely related to the concept of swing, which had something to do with the characteristic placement of musical details against a metronomic underpinning of regular stresses. The origins of jazz as dance music are of importance here. Thanks largely to Ornette Coleman, Charles Mingus, and the black avant-garde, the treatment of rhythm and meter in jazz was substantially enhanced. These leaders demonstrated that jazz did not have to "swing" in the traditional manner; in the process, the rhythm section was emancipated from its traditional duties. Accordingly, the rhythm section of much post-sixties jazz — be it the conventional piano, drums set, and string bass or an arsenal of percussion instruments — participates in the music-making in a much different spirit. The contributions of the later rhythm sections are typically much more complex. The swing concept, of course, did not disappear, but after the sixties, it was no longer a binding condition on all jazz.

The elimination of the "standard" popular song as the jazz musician's theme for variation represents yet another dramatic departure from the established practice, especially from the standpoint of listeners. Traditionally a primary source of satisfaction for them had been hearing how individual jazz artists rendered familiar material. Listeners were able to judge both the technical and the creative gifts of artists because of their prior knowledge of the theme. Improvised solos were related often to the melody, but always to the harmony. When some jazz musicians rejected the popular song as a basis for their improvisations in the early sixties, they removed this important point of reference for listeners. Original material, customarily created by reformers and often musically challenging, was presented as the alternative theme. To compound the difficulty, the improvisations in such cases were only loosely connected with statements of the original theme — if at all — placing listeners at a considerable disadvantage. Throughout its history, jazz musicians have typically included original pieces in their repertories, but since the sixties it has become almost obligatory for musicians to create their own tunes and to present them as new themes in performances. The vast majority of these musical subjects are never taken up by other artists. Thus, the members of the jazz audience in the post-sixties era have been given musical responsibilities of a drastically different kind. The close relationship that had existed between American popular music and the contemporaneous jazz tradition was no longer in force. Although numerous jazz musicians have made conspicuous borrowings from the popular music tradition after the sixties, notably aspects of rock and roll, the treatment of the current popular song (in the form of rock and roll) as the theme for jazz variations is no longer the norm.

Other factors that tend to distinguish a second practice (post-sixties) from a first practice (pre-sixties) may be cited. Electronic instruments and electronically-altered sound, introduced during the sixties, remain fundamentally important to the jazz world. There is no reason not to believe that the computer and the synthesizer have great potential in the jazz context. Moreover, to a far greater degree than before 1960, concert performances before huge audiences, in other words the institutionalization of "arena jazz," has been made feasible by electronically amplified sound and other technologies. One might suppose that before 1960, more people heard live jazz in a nightclub or dance hall than a concert setting; the opposite seems true for the period following the sixties.

One final point of distinction between the two proposed phases of jazz history may be made by considering a time-honored ritual, the jam session. During the first phase the idea of a jam session presented few problems for leading musicians. Each was conversant with the current style, techniques, and repertory. Musicians who had never played together before could, and did, collaborate with felicitous results. A jam session with established musicians during the second phase, on the other hand, might very well prove to be an embarrassment, if not a musical disaster. The absence of common experience — other than the blues, perhaps — and of common approaches might represent obstacles that would be insurmountable.[6]

These observations, as well as the opinions of Leonard Feather and Max Harrison cited above, lead to another thought-

provoking hypothesis. It is possible that the revolutionary passion of the sixties and its various products served as a prelude to
a period of stylistic "stasis" in jazz. This concept is borrowed
from music theorist Leonard B. Meyer, who has perceived both
the conditions for such a state of affairs in contemporary culture
and its reflection in the creative arts. He defines the phenomenon as "the persistence over a considerable period of time of . . .
a steady-state in which an indefinite number of styles and idioms, techniques and movements, will coexist. . . . There will be
no central, common practice, . . . no stylistic 'victory.'"[7] Meyer's
definition of stasis appears to be a faithful characterization of
developments in the jazz tradition after the sixties. One passage
from his landmark text *Music, the Arts, and Ideas: Patterns and Predictions in Twentieth-Century Culture* (1967) seems particularly relevant in this discussion of recent jazz:

> More specifically, with references to the arts, discovery is
> no longer a real possibility. By and large the arts of other
> cultures, past and present, are available on phonograph
> records, in translations of literature and philosophy, and in
> museums or in reproductions. The artist need only choose
> his source of influence. Both the cultural present and the
> cultural past are from this point of view timeless and static.[8]

In light of this thought, one might argue that the conservation
of past and present accomplishments has been adopted as the
prevailing aesthetic priority in the jazz world out of some necessity and that the musicians and their audiences are no longer
seeking or expecting dramatic change. This assessment does not
preclude the idea of novelty in future jazz, but it does suggest
that the tradition need not be driven by a constant search for
new modes of expression. A compelling part of Meyer's argument is his evidence that only in Western civilization has the idea
of relentless change received such a high premium and that the
conditions for this preference have gradually diminished in the
West. Most of the world's musical cultures traditionally have
placed emphasis on stability and continuity.[9]

In other words, since the sixties, it has become artistically
viable to make jazz according to many of the pre-ordained styles
in its rather large historical museum. Collective improvisation

can flourish alongside paraphrased versions of popular songs by Irving Berlin or Stevie Wonder. Fusion music need not compete with big-band arrangements in a tight, swing style. Piano jazz with a Latin beat can co-exist with the descendents of Art Tatum and the imitators of Keith Jarrett. The durable popularity of legendary performances from the past is handily accommodated by such an aesthetic point of view. In short, since the sixties, a well-established universe of jazz styles — in both live and recorded formats — has been constantly embraced by the jazz-loving public. The application of Meyer's theory to what has been described here as the second phase in jazz history seems remarkably appropriate.

One last interpretation for consideration makes use of a human metaphor for jazz. It may be instructive to perceive the sixties as a kind of "coming of age" for jazz. The single line of stylistic evolution from its beginning might be considered as phases of development in a growth process similar but not necessarily functionally analogous to the infancy, childhood, and adolescence of a human being. The period of experimentation and reevaluation exhibited in the sixties, accordingly, might be likened to the first freedom of adulthood, when the individual, filled with self-confidence and aware of his or her own powers, feels compelled to test the status quo and to come to terms with his or her own nature. The exploration is sometimes marked by excesses, even indiscretions, but it remains an essentially inevitable and invaluable experience. Unable to sustain itself, such intensity is then replaced with a studied knowledge of the possibilities and, now with tolerance for the views of others, a return to what is truly workable, durable, and meaningful.

Perceiving the history of jazz in this manner has several advantages. It does no disservice or dishonor to the enthusiastic appreciation of earlier sub-styles to understand them as conceptual points along an evolutionary continuum. After all, evolution is a matter of changing priorities and should not be necessarily related to the idea of progress, which implies a succession of improvements. One of the glories of jazz history is the very fact that these changes have been documented on recordings. At the same time, however, it is imperative to emphasize that the first sixty or so years of jazz, with the rapid changes in style, witnessed a decided enrichment in the nature and treatment of musical materials and, as a result, a substantial increase in the technical demands made on the improvising artist. Since the sixties the technical prowess of a great majority of jazz musicians, including those with only local or regional reputations, has been admirably high, and a corresponding versatility — the practical knowledge of several styles — has grown to satisfy the trend toward pluralism.

Throughout its short history, the music known as jazz has invariably reached out to touch the soul and challenge the mind, and jazz musicians during the sixties produced their fair share of emotionally charged and intellectually stimulating performances. Like all human endeavors, much of this music deserves its day in the sun before passing into oblivion, but the best of it becomes a part of who we are. Music is valuable because of the meanings assigned to it — as personal expression, as social discourse, as emotional stimulant, as intellectual exploration. The jazz that endures from that extraordinarily productive era will surely communicate the intensity of the quest and the excitement of enriching the tradition. The stylistic leap taken by the leading jazz figures of that time may not be repeated for some time to come.

---

1   See Max Harrison, "Jazz," *The New Grove Gospel, Blues and Jazz* (New York: Macmillan, 1986), pp. 316–22.

2   Leonard Feather, record liner notes to *Odyssey of Iska* by Wayne Shorter (Blue Note 84363, 1970).

3   Quoted without documentation in James Lincoln Collier, *The Making of Jazz* (Boston: Houghton Mifflin, 1978), p. 496.

4   Harrison, "Jazz," *The New Grove Gospel, Blues and Jazz*, p. 334.

5   Harrison, "Jazz," *The New Grove Gospel, Blues and Jazz*, p. 334, characterizes Coleman's work as setting the stage for "a completely new and independent beginning" for jazz, but suggests that this promise was not fulfilled. On the other hand, John Litweiler, *The Freedom Principle: Jazz after 1958* (New York: William Morrow, 1984), has written an entire book describing the music that has sprung from Coleman's "free" approach beginning in 1958.

6   Litweiler, *The Freedom Principle*, p. 287, makes a similar assertion about a hypothetical jam session with leading free-jazz musicians; he contends that they often share no common ground.

7   Leonard B. Meyer, *Music, the Arts, and Ideas: Patterns and Predic-*

tions in *Twentieth-Century Culture* (Chicago: University of Chicago Press, 1967), p. 172.

8 *Ibid.*, 136.

9 See especially Meyer, "As It Is, and Perhaps Will Be," in *Music, The Arts, and Ideas*, pp. 87–232. He addresses the following topics: "History, Stasis, and Change," "Varieties of Style Change," "The Probability of Stasis," and "The Aesthetics of Stasis."

Appendix: Discography of Recordings Cited

In the following list of recordings cited in the text, the entries are arranged alphabetically according to the last name of the leader of the ensemble. When several recordings by the same artist appear, they are presented in chronological order.

Abrams, Richard. *Levels and Degrees of Light*. Delmark 413, 1968.

Almeida, Laurindo & Bud Shank. *Holiday in Brazil*. World Pacific WP-1259, 1959.

Art Ensemble of Chicago. *Les Stances a Sophie*. Nessa N-4, 1970.

Brubeck, Dave. *Time Out*. Columbia CS-8192, 1960.

———. *Time Further Out*. Columbia CS-8490, 1961.

———. *Time Changes*. Columbia CS-2127, 1964.

Carlos, Walter. *Switched-on Bach*. Columbia MS-7194, 1968.

Coleman, Ornette. *The Shape of Jazz to Come*. Atlantic 1317, 1959.

———. *Change of the Century*. Atlantic 1327, 1959.

———. *Free Jazz*. Atlantic 1364, 1960.

———. *Plays with the Master Musicians of Joujouka, Morocco*.

Coltrane, Alice. *Journey in Satchidananda*. Impulse AS-9203, 1970.

Coltrane, John. *Giant Steps*. Atlantic 1311, 1960.

———. *My Favorite Things*. Atlantic 1361, 1960.

———. *Impressions*. Impulse AS-42, 1961/63.

———. *Live at Birdland*. Impulse AS-50, 1963.

———. *A Love Supreme*. Impulse S-77, 1964.

———. *Ascension*. Impulse AS-95, 1965.

———. *Meditations*. Impulse AS–9110, 1966.

Davis, Miles. *Milestones*. Columbia CS–1193, 1958.

———. *Kind of Blue*. Columbia CS–8163, 1959.

———. *ESP*. Columbia CS–9150, 1965.

———. *Miles in the Sky*. Columbia CS–9628, 1968.

———. *In a Silent Way*. Columbia CS–9875, 1969.

———. *Bitches Brew*. Columbia 2–GP 26, 1969.

———. *A Tribute to Jack Johnson*. Columbia CS KC–30455, 1970.

———. *Live-Evil*. Columbia G–30954, 1970.

———. *Big Fun*. Columbia PG–32866, 1969/70/72.

Desmond, Paul. *Bossa Antigua*. Victor LPM–3320, 1965.

Dolphy, Eric. *Eric Dolphy in Europe*. Vol. 1. Prestige PR–7304, 1963.

Ellington, Duke. *A Concert of Sacred Music*. RCA Victor LSP–3582, 1966.

———. *New Orleans Suite*. Atlantic SD–1580, 1971.

———. *Second Sacred Concert*. Prestige P–24045, n.d.

Ellis, Don. *How Time Passes*. Candid 8004, 1961.

———. *Live at Monterrey*. Pacific Jazz 20112, 1965.

———. *Live in 3⅔/4 Time*. Pacific Jazz PJ–10123, 1967.

———. *Electric Bath*. Columbia CS–9585, 1968.

———. *At Fillmore*. Columbia CG–30243, 1970.

Evans, Bill. *The Bill Evans Album*. Columbia C–30855, 1971.

Getz, Stan. *Big Band Bossa Nova*. Verve V–8494, 1962.

Getz, Stan & Charlie Byrd. *Jazz Samba*. Verve 8432, 1962.

Getz, Stan & João Gilberto. *Getz-Gilberto*. Verve 8545, 1964.

Gilberto, João. *Chega de Saudade*. Odeon MOFB–3073, 1959.

Hancock, Herbie. *Maiden Voyage*. Blue Note BLP–4195/84195, 1965.

Horn, Paul. *Jazz Suite on the Mass Text*. RCA Victor LPM–3414, 1965.

———. *Paul Horn in India*. World Pacific WPS–21447, 1967.

———. *Paul Horn in Kashmir*. World Pacific WPS–1445, 1967.

Jarman, Joseph. *Song For*. Delmark 410. 1967.

Jones, Thad & Mel Lewis. *Central Park North*. Solid State 18058, 1969.

Kenton, Stan. *Artistry in Bossa Nova*. Capitol T–1931, 1963.

———. *Conducts the Los Angeles Neophonic Orchestra*. Capitol MAS–2424, 1965.

Lateef, Yusef. *1984*. Impulse S–84, 1966.

Lloyd, Charles. Forest Flower. Atlantic S–1473, 1967.

Mann, Herbie. *Do the Bossa Nova*. Atlantic 1397, 1963.

McLaughlin, John. *Birds of Fire*. Columbia KC–31996, 1973.

Mingus, Charles. *The Clown*. Atlantic 1260, 1957.

———. *Charles Mingus Presents Charles Mingus*. America AM–6082, 1960.

———. *The Black Saint and the Sinner Lady*. Impulse AS–35, 1963.

Modern Jazz Quartet. *European Concert*. Atlantic 2–603, 1960.

———. *Third Stream Music*. Atlantic 1345, 1960.

Nelson, Oliver. *Sound Pieces*. Impulse S–9129, 1967.

———. *Afro/American Sketches*. Prestige 7225, 1961.

Ponty, Jean-Luc & Sahib Shihab. *Jazz Meets Arabia: Noon in Tunisia*. BASF/MPS ST–20640, 1966.

Roach, Max. *We Insist: Freedom Now Suite*. Candid 8002, 1960.

Schifrin, Lalo. *Bossa Nova*. Audio Fidelity AF–5981, 1962.

Shankar, Ravi. *Portrait of Genius*. World Pacific WPS–1432, 1965.

Shepp, Archie. *Fire Music*. Impulse AS–86, 1965.

———. *Live at the Pan-African Festival*. Actuel 51, 1969.

Sun Ra. *The Heliocentric World of Sun Ra*. Vol. 1. ESP–1014, 1965.

———. *Nuits de la Fondation Maeght*. Vol. 1. Shandar SR–10.001, 1970.

Taylor, Cecil. *Unit Structures*. Blue Note 84237, 1966.

Thomas, Leon. *Spirits Known and Unknown*. Flying Dutchman 10115, 1974.

Various artists. *Jazz Abstractions*. Atlantic 1365, 1961.

———. *New Wave in Jazz*. Impulse A–90, 1965.

Williams, Tony. *Emergency!* Polydor 25–3001, 1970.

Winter, Paul. *The Sound of Ipanema*. Columbia CS–9072, 1964.

———. *Rio*. Columbia CS–9115, 1965.

ADDENDA

Brubeck, Dave. *Jazz Impressions of Japan*. Columbia PC 9012, 1964.

Davis, Miles, and Gil Evans. *Sketches of Spain*. Columbia CL 1480, 1960.

Ellington, Duke. *Third Sacred Concert*. RCA SF 8406, 1973.

———. *The Far East Suite*. LPM/LSP–3782, 1966; reissued Bluebird 7640–1–RB, 1988.

Rollins, Sonny. *Freedom Suite*. Riverside OJC–067/RLP–258, 1958.

Shepp, Archie. *Four for Trane*. Impulse AS–71, 1964.

Shepp, Archie, and Philly Joe Jones. *The Lowlands*. Fantasy 86018, 1969.

Shorter, Wayne. *Odyssey of Iska*. Blue Note 84363, 1970.

Tyner, McCoy. *Extensions*. Blue Note LA006G, 1970.

Bibliography

GENERAL WORKS ON JAZZ AND RELATED TOPICS

Baker, David N. "A Periodization of Black Music History." In *Reflections on Afro-American Music*. Edited by Dominique-René de Lerma. Kent, Ohio: Kent State University Press, 1973.

Barlow, Wayne. "Electronic Music: Challenge to Music Education." *Music Educators Journal* 53 (November 1968), 66–69.

Baskerville, David Ross. "Jazz Influence on Art Music to Mid-Century." Ph.D. dissertation, University of California, Los Angeles, 1965.

Bebey, Francis. *African Music: A People's Art.* Translated by Josephine Bennett. New York: Lawrence Hill, 1975.

Berendt, Joachim-Ernst. *The Jazz Book: From New Orleans to Rock and Free Jazz.* Translated by Dan Morgenstern, Helmut Bredigkeit & Barbara Bredigkeit. New York: Lawrence Hill, 1975.

Boeckman, Charles. *Cool, Hot and Blue: A History of Jazz for Young People.* Washington, D.C.: Luce, 1968.

Coker, Jerry. *Improvising Jazz.* Englewood Cliffs, N.J.: Prentice-Hall, 1964.

Collier, Graham. *Inside Jazz.* London: Quartet, 1973.

———. *Jazz: A Student's and Teacher's Guide.* The Resources of Music Series, edited by Wilfrid Mellers and John Paynter, vol. 10. London: Cambridge University Press, 1975.

Dallin, Leon. *Techniques of Twentieth Century Composition*, 3d ed. Dubuque, Iowa: Wm. C. Brown, 1974.

Daniélou, Alain. "The Musical Languages of Black Africa." In *African Music.* Paris: La Revue Musicale, 1972.

Feather, Leonard. *The Book of Jazz from Then till Now: A Guide to the Entire Field.* Rev. ed. New York: Bonanza, 1965.

———. *The Encyclopedia of Jazz.* New ed. New York: Bonanza, 1960.

————. *From Satchmo to Miles.* New York: Stein & Day, 1972.

Gillenson, Lewis W., ed. *Esquire's World of Jazz.* New York: Thomas Y. Crowell, 1975.

Gleason, Ralph. *Celebrating the Duke and Others.* New York: Little, Brown, 1975.

Goldberg, Joe. *Jazz Masters of the Fifties.* New York: Macmillan, 1965.

Green, Benny. "The World of Jazz." In *Larousse Encyclopedia of Music.* Edited by Antony Hopkins. London: Hamlyn, 1971.

Helm, Sanford Marion. "Jazz: Music History in Miniature." *Music Educators Journal* 51 (February 1965), 53.

Hentoff, Nat. *The Jazz Life.* New York: Dial, 1961.

Jones, A. M. *Studies in African Music.* London: Oxford University Press, 1959.

Jones, LeRoi. *Blues People: The Negro Experience in White America and the Music that Developed from It.* New York: Morrow, 1963.

Kebede, Ashenafi. "African Music in the Western Hemisphere." In *African Music.* Paris: La Revue Musicale, 1972.

Krähenbühl, Peter. *Der Jazz und seine Menschen: Eine soziologische Studie.* Bern: Francke, 1968.

Lee, Edward. *Jazz: An Introduction.* London: Kahn & Averill, 1972.

Marcuse, Sybil. *Musical Instruments: A Comprehensive Dictionary.* Garden City, N.Y.: Doubleday, 1971.

McCarthy, Albert, Alun Morgan, Paul Oliver, and Max Harrison. *Jazz on Record: A Critical Guide to the First 50 Years, 1917–1967.* London: Hanover, 1968.

Mehegan, John. *Jazz Improvisation.* 4 vols. New York: Watson-Guptill, 1959–65.

Mellers, Wilfrid. *Music in a New Found Land: Themes and Developments in the History of American Music.* London: Barrie & Rockliff, 1964.

Morgenstern, Dan. "Jazz Fiddle: From Venuti and South to Ponty and Ornette — A Survey of Those Who Play." *down beat* 34 (February 9, 1967), 16–19, 38.

Nanry, Charles, ed. *American Music: From Storyville to Woodstock.* New Brunswick: Transaction, 1972.

Nye, Russell. *The Unembarrassed Muse: The Popular Arts in America.* Two Centuries of American Life, edited by Harold M. Hyman and Leonard W. Levy. New York: Dial, 1970.

Palmer, Robert. Record liner notes to *The Saxophone: A Critical Analytic Guide to the Major Trends in the Development of the Contemporary Saxophone Tradition.* By various artists. Impulse ASH–9253–3, 1973.

Pleasants, Henry. *Death of a Music?* London: Gollancz, 1961.

———. *Serious Music — and All That Jazz.* London: Gollancz, 1969.

Russell, George Allan. *The Lydian Chromatic Concept of Tonal Organization.* New York: Concept, 1953.

Russo, William. *Jazz Composition and Orchestration.* Chicago: University of Chicago Press, 1968.

Sargeant, Winthrop. *Jazz: A History.* New York: McGraw-Hill, 1964.

Schuller, Gunther. *Early Jazz: Its Roots and Musical Development.* The History of Jazz, 1. New York: Oxford University Press, 1968.

Sidran, Ben. *Black Talk.* New York: Holt, Rinehart & Winston, 1971.

Slonimsky, Nicolas, ed. *Music Since 1900.* 4th ed. New York: Scribner, 1971.

Southern, Eileen. *The Music of Black Americans: A History.* New York: Norton, 1971.

———. *Readings in Black American Music.* New York: Norton, 1972.

Stambler, Irwin. *Encyclopedia of Pop, Rock & Soul.* New York: St. Martin's Press, 1974.

Stearns, Marshall W. *The Story of Jazz.* New York: Oxford University Press, 1956.

Tanner, Paul O. W. and Maurice Gerow. *A Study of Jazz.* 2d ed. Dubuque, Iowa: Wm. C. Brown, 1973.

Tirro, Frank. "Constructive Elements in Jazz Improvisation." *Journal of the American Musicological Society* 27 (Summer 1974), 285–305.

———. "Jazz." In *Dictionary of Contemporary Music.* Edited by John Vinton. New York: Dutton, 1971.

———. "The Silent Theme Tradition." *Musical Quarterly* 53 (1967), 313–34.

White, John Reeves and André Boucourechliev. "Aleatory Music." In

Harvard Dictionary of Music. 2d ed. Edited by Willi Apel. Cambridge, Mass.: Belknap, 1969.

Williams, Martin T. *The Jazz Tradition.* New York: Oxford University Press, 1970.

————. *The Smithsonian Collection of Classic Jazz.* Washington, D.C.: Smithsonian Institution, 1973. (Supplementary booklet.)

Wilson, John S. *Jazz: The Transition Years, 1940–1960.* New York: Appleton-Century-Crofts, 1966.

STUDIES OF JAZZ IN THE SIXTIES

General Works

Balliett, Whitney. *Dinosaurs in the Morning: Forty-one Pieces on Jazz.* Philadelphia: Lippincott, 1962.

————. *Ecstasy at the Onion: Thirty-one Pieces on Jazz.* New York: Bobbs-Merrill, 1972.

————. *Such Sweet Thunder: Forty-nine Pieces on Jazz.* Indianapolis: Bobbs-Merrill, 1966.

Feather, Leonard. *The Encyclopedia of Jazz in the Sixties.* New York: Bonanza, 1966.

Gonda, Janos. "Problems of Tonality and Function in Modern Jazz Improvisation." *Jazzforschung* 3 (1971–72), 194–205.

Larkin, Phillip. *All What Jazz: A Record Diary, 1961–68.* New York: St. Martin's Press, 1970.

McRae, Barry. *The Jazz Cataclysm.* South Brunswick, N.J.: A. S. Barnes, 1967.

Morgenstern, Dan. "Jazz Today." In *Esquire's World of Jazz.* Edited by Lewis W. Gillenson. New York: Thomas Y. Crowell, 1975.

Schreiner, Claus. *Jazz Aktuell.* Mainz: Schott, 1968.

Stearns, Marshall. "Main Trends in Jazz Today." *Musical America* 81 (1961), 22–23.

Williams, Martin T. *Jazz Masters in Transition, 1957–1969.* London: Collier-Macmillan, 1970.

The Avant-Garde and Black Nationalism

Clarke, Carl. "Notes on the New Thing." *Library Journal* 93 (April 15, 1968), 61–64.

Charles, Philippe and Jean-Louis Comolli. *Free Jazz/Black Power.* Paris: Editions Champs Libre, 1971.

Erskine, Gilbert and Bill Mathieu. "Two Views of the New Wave." *down beat* 33 (January 27, 1966), 29–30.

Heckman, Don. "Caught in the Act: The Jazz Composers Guild." *down beat* 32 (February 11, 1965), 37–38.

———. "The New Jazz: A Matter of Doing." *down beat* 34 (February 9, 1967), 24–25.

Hentoff, Nat. "The New Jazz: Black, Angry, and Hard to Understand." *New York Times Magazine* (December 25, 1966), 28–32.

Hodeir, André. "Free Jazz." *World of Music* 10 (1968), 20–29.

Hunt, D. C. "Coleman, Coltrane and Shepp: The Need for an Educated Audience." *Jazz & Pop* 7 (October 1968), 18–21.

———. "Speech-inflected Jazz, Rhythm-dominated Jazz Plus Other Influences." *Jazz & Pop* 9 (August 1970), 32–34.

Jones, LeRoi. *Black Music.* New York: Morrow, 1967.

———. "Apple Cores: Strong Voices in Today's Black Music." *down beat* 33 (February 10, 1966), 15.

Jones, LeRoi and Steve Young. Record liner notes to *The New Wave in Jazz.* By various artists. Impulse AS–90, 1965.

Jost, Ekkehard. *Free Jazz.* Beiträge zur Jazzforschung, edited by Friedrich Körner and Dieter Glawischnig. Graz: Universal, 1974.

———. "Free Jazz und die Musik der Dritten Welt." *Jazzforschung* 3 (1971–72), 141–54.

Kofsky, Frank. *Black Nationalism and the Revolution in Music.* New York: Pathfinder, 1970.

Korall, Burt. "The Music of Protest." *Saturday Review* 51 (November 16, 1968), 36.

Levin, Robert. "The Jazz Composers Guild: An Assertion of Dignity." *down beat* 32 (May 6, 1965), 17–18.

Matzorkis, Gus. "Down Where We Live: Today's Avant-Garde Revolution as Seen in Light of Jazz's Long History of Internal Strife" I.

down beat 33 (April 7, 1966), 21–22; II. *down beat* 33 (April 21, 1966), 17–18.

Miller, Lloyd and James K. Skipper, Jr. "Sounds of Black Protest in Avant Garde Jazz." In *Sounds of Social Change*. Edited by R. Serge Denisoff and Richard A. Peterson. Chicago: Rand McNally, 1972.

Morgenstern, Dan and Martin T. Williams. "The October Revolution: Two Views of the Avant Garde in Action." *down beat* 31 (November 19, 1964), 15.

Palmer, Robert. "Clifford Thornton: Flowers in the Garden of Harlem." *down beat* 42 (June 19, 1975), 19.

Pekar, Harvey. "Experimental Collective Improvisation." *Jazz Journal* 16 (November 1963), 8–9.

Reeve, Stephen. "The New Piano in the New Jazz." *Jazz Journal* 22 (September 1969), 25.

Welding, Pete. "Caught in the Act: Joseph Jarman — John Cage." *down beat* 33 (January 13, 1966), 35–36.

The Bossa Nova and Brazilian Instruments

Alvarenga, Oneyda. *Música popular brasileña*. Buenos Aires: Fondo de Cultura Economica, 1947.

Balliett, Whitney. "Bossa Nova, Go Home." *New Yorker* 39 (December 1, 1962), 197–99.

Béhague, Gerard. "Bossa & Bossas: Recent Changes in Brazilian Urban Popular Music." *Ethnomusicology* 17 (1973), 209–33.

Cerulli, Dom. Record liner notes to *Jazz Samba* by Stan Getz and Charlie Byrd. Verve 8432, 1962.

Galm, John K. "How to Perk Up Percussion." *down beat* 42 (December 4, 1975), 36–37.

Grant, Felix. Record liner notes to *The Sound of Ipanema* by Paul Winter. Columbia CS–9072, 1964.

Moraes, Vinícius de. Record liner notes to *Rio* by Paul Winter. Columbia CS–9115, 1965.

Rivelli, Pauline. A review of *Do the Bossa Nova* by Herbie Mann (Atlantic 1397, 1963). In *Jazz* 2 (March 1963), 25.

Shaw, Arnold. "The Dilemma of Jazz." *Jazz* 4 (April 1965), 8–11.

Sinzig, Frei Pedro. *Dicionarário musical.* 2d ed. Rio de Janeiro: Livraria Kosmos Editora, 1959.

Thompson, Robert Farris. "The 'Bossa Nova' from Brazil." *Saturday Review* 45 (September 15, 1962), 42–43.

———. "Bossa Nova from the Source." *Saturday Review* 47 (July 11, 1964), 42–43.

———. "Bossa Up to Date." *Saturday Review* 48 (November 13, 1965), 80–81.

Taylor, James L. *A Portuguese-English Dictionary.* Stanford: Stanford University Press, 1959.

Tynan, John A. "The Real Story of the Bossa Nova." *down beat* 29 (November 8, 1962), 21–22.

Welding, Pete. "Bossa Nova Bevy." *down beat* 32 (May 6, 1965), 27.

Williams, Martin T. "Bossa from Both Sides of the Border." *Saturday Review* 46 (February 23, 1963), 57.

———. "Whose Bossa?" In *Jazz Masters in Transition, 1957–1969.* New York: Macmillan, 1970.

Electronic Instruments

Fowler, William L. "How to Electrify a Horn and an Audience." *down beat* 41 (July 18, 1974), 42.

Gardner, Barbara. "The Electrified Sonny Stitt," *down beat* 33 (October 6, 1966), 16–17.

Rhea, Thomas LaMar. "The Evolution of Electronic Musical Instruments in the United States." Ph.D. dissertation, George Peabody College for Teachers, 1972.

Strange, Allen. *Electronic Music: Systems, Techniques, and Controls.* Dubuque, Iowa: Wm. C. Brown, 1972.

The Influence of Indian Music

Berendt, Joachim-Ernst. "Jazz Meets the World." *World of Music* 10 (1968), 8–19.

Ellis, Don and Hari Har Rao. "An Introduction to Indian Music for the Jazz Musician." *Jazz* 4 (April 1965), 20–22.

Handy, John Williams. "Caught in the Act: Hindustani Jazz Sextet." *down beat* 32 (November 18, 1965), 34–35.

Kaufmann, Walter. "India." In *Harvard Dictionary of Music*. 2d ed. Edited by Willi Apel. Cambridge, Mass.: Belknap, 1969.

————. *The Ragas of North India*. Bloomington, Ind.: Indiana University Press, 1968.

Mayer, John. "Indo-Jazz Fusions." *Composer* 34 (Winter 1969–70), 5.

Palmer, Robert. Record liner notes to *Paul Horn in India* by Paul Horn. Blue Note LA529–H2, 1975.

Siders, Harvey. "Caught in the Act: Los Angeles Neophonic Orchestra." *down beat* 33 (March 24, 1966), 47–48.

Tynan, John A. "India's Master Musician: Ravi Shankar." *down beat* 32 (May 6, 1965), 14.

The Influence of Rock

Gibbs, Vernon. "Tony Williams: Report on a Musical Lifetime." *down beat* 43 (January 29, 1976), 16–18.

Goldman, Albert. "Jazz Meets Rock." *Atlantic Monthly* 208 (February 1971), 98–106.

Heckman, Don. "Jazz — Rock." *Stereo Review* 33 (November 1974), 74–78.

Kamin, Jonathan. "Parallels in the Social Reaction to Jazz and Rock." *Journal of Jazz Studies* 2 (December 1974), 95–125.

Levin, Robert. "Notes on the Jazz Syndrome." In *Rock '71*. Edited by Chris Hodenfield. New York: Pyramid, 1970.

Palmer, Robert. "Jazz Rock." In *The Rolling Stone Illustrated History of Rock & Roll*. Edited by Jim Miller. New York: Random House, 1976.

Schaffer, Jim. "Mahavishnu's Apocalypse." *down beat* 41 (June 6, 1974), 14.

Serialism in Jazz

Banks, Don. "Converging Streams." *Musical Times* 111 (June 1970), 596–99.

Binkley, Fred. Record liner notes to *The Bill Evans Album* by Bill Evans. Columbia C–30855, 1971.

Brown, Robert L. "Classical Influences on Jazz." *Journal of Jazz Studies* 3 (Spring 1976), 19–35.

Feather, Leonard. "Twelve Tone Blues." *down beat* 33 (February 24, 1966), 17.

Heckman, Don. "Sounds and Silence: 12-Tone Music." *down beat* 33 (June 30, 1966), 26–27.

Schuller, Gunther. Record liner notes to *Jazz Abstractions* by various artists. Atlantic 1365, 1961.

Third Stream Music

Balliett, Whitney. "Third Stream." In *Dinosaurs in the Morning: Forty-one Pieces on Jazz*. Philadelphia: Lippincott, 1962.

Blatny, Pavel. "Was kann der Jazz der Neuen Musik geben? Was kann die Neue Musik dem Jazz geben?" *Jazzforschung* 3 (1971–72), 217–24.

Crickmore, Leon. "Third Stream or Third Programme?" *Musical Times* 102 (November 1961), 701–02.

DeMichael, Don. "Structure and Freedom: A Reappraisal of the Modern Jazz Quartet." *down beat* 32 (June 17, 1965), 24.

Denissow, Edison. "New Music and Jazz." *World of Music* 10 (1968), 30–37.

Dommett, Kenneth. "Jazz and the Composer." *Proceedings of the Royal Musical Association* 91 (1964–65), 11–20.

Feather, Leonard. "Caught in the Act: Los Angeles Neophonic Orchestra." *down beat* 33 (February 24, 1966), 36.

Goldberg, Joe. "The Third Stream: Is It Killing Jazz? — Yes." *Hifi/Stereo Review* 7 (July 1961), 45.

Gower, Patrick. "Modern Jazz." *Musical Times* 103 (June 1962), 389–92.

Harrison, Max. Record liner notes to *Third Stream Music* by the Modern Jazz Quartet, Jimmy Giuffre Three and Beaux Arts String Quartet. Atlantic 1345, 1960.

Heckman, Don. "Caught in the Act: Orchestra U.S.A." *down beat* 32 (January 14, 1965), 31–32.

Hentoff, Nat. "The Third Stream." *International Musician* 60 (October 1961), 24–25.

————. "The Third Stream: Is It Killing Jazz? — No." *Hifi-Stereo Review* 7 (July 1961), 44.

Hunt, Daniel S. "Jazz Plus Classical: A Third Stream Music?" *Music Journal* 20 (February 1962), 36.

Lees, Gene. "Views of the Third Stream." *down beat* 31 (February 13, 1964), 16–17.

Levine, Evelyn. Record liner notes to *In Memoriam* by the Modern Jazz Quartet with orchestra. Little David LD 3001, 1974.

Mitchell, Sunny. "Third Stream Visitation: A Talk with Gunther Schuller." *down beat* 35 (February 22, 1968), 20–21.

Pleasants, Henry. "Jazz and Classical." *Jazz* 2 (Spring 1959), 88–94.

Robinson, Leroy. "Neophonic Contrasts." *Jazz* 4 (April 1965), 29–30.

Russo, William. "Jazz and Classical Music." In *The New Yearbook of Jazz*. Edited by Leonard Feather. New York: Horizon, 1958.

Schuller, Gunther. "The Future of Form in Jazz." In *The American Composer Speaks: A Historical Anthology, 1770–1965*. Edited by Gilbert Chase. Baton Rouge, La.: Louisiana State University Press, 1966.

————. "Jazz and Classical Music." In *The Encyclopedia of Jazz*. New ed. Edited by Leonard Feather. New York: Bonanza, 1960.

————. Record liner notes to *Jazz Abstractions: Compositions of Gunther Schuller and Jim Hall* by various artists. Atlantic 1365, 1961.

————. "'Third Stream' Redefined." *Saturday Review* 44 (May 13, 1961), 54–55.

Siders, Harvey. "Caught in the Act: Los Angeles Neophonic Orchestra." *down beat* 33 (March 24, 1966), 47–48.

————. "Caught in the Act: Los Angeles Neophonic Orchestra." *down beat* 32 (May 20, 1965), 34.

Slonimsky, Nicolas, ed. "Third Stream." In *Music Since 1900*. 4th ed. New York: Scribner, 1971.

Smith, Charles Edward. "Jazz Parallels: Third Stream." *Jazz* 5 (October 1966), 14.

Tynan, John A. "Caught in the Act: Los Angeles Neophonic Orchestra." *down beat* 32 (February 25, 1965), 15.

————. "Caught in the Act: Los Angeles Neophonic Orchestra," *down beat* 32 (May 20, 1965), 34.

————. "Stan Kenton's Neophonic Music." *down beat* 32 (January 14, 1965), 12–15.

Williams, Martin T. "Jazz Composition." *down beat* 29 (February 15, 1962), 20–23.

————. "Problems in the Third Stream." *Jazz* 4 (January 1965), 12.

————. "Third Stream Problems." In *Jazz Masters in Transition, 1957–1969*. New York: Macmillan, 1970.

STUDIES OF INDIVIDUAL MUSICIANS

Albert Ayler

Hentoff, Nat. "The Truth Is Marching On: An Interview with Albert and Don Ayler." *down beat* 33 (November 17, 1966), 16.

Kofsky, Frank. "The Case of Albert Ayler." *Jazz* 5 (September 1966), 24–25; *Jazz* 5 (October 1966), 20–22.

Smith, Frank. "His Name Is Albert Ayler." *Jazz* (December 1965), 11–14.

Woodfin, Henry. "Whither Albert Ayler?" *down beat* 33 (November 17, 1966), 19.

Ornette Coleman

Bourne, Michael. "Ornette's Interview." *down beat* 40 (November 22, 1973), 16–17.

Coleman, Ornette. Record liner notes to *Change of the Century* by Ornette Coleman. Atlantic 1327, 1959.

Heckman, Don. "Ornette and the Sixties." *down beat* 31 (July 2, 1964), 58–62.

————. "Ornette Coleman and the Quiet Revolution." *Saturday Review* 46 (January 12, 1963), 78–79.

Jost, Ekkehard. "Zur Musik Ornette Colemans." *Jazzforschung* 2 (1970), 105–24.

McRae, Barry. "Avant Courier: Kaleidoscope." *Jazz Journal* 26 (February 1973), 10.

————. "Avant Courier: The Ornette Coleman Atlantics." *Jazz Journal* 28 (April 1975), 14–16.

Russell, George and Martin T. Williams. "Ornette Coleman and Tonality." *Jazz Review* 3 (June 1960), 6–10.

Spellman, A. B. "Ornette Coleman." In *Black Music: Four Lives.* 2d ed. New York: Schocken, 1970.

Williams, Martin T. "Ornette Coleman: A New Kind of Jazz Improvising." *Jazz* 2 (November 1963), 24–25.

————. "Ornette Coleman: Ten Years After." *down beat* 36 (December 25, 1969), 24–25.

————. Record liner notes to *Free Jazz* by Ornette Coleman. Atlantic 1364, 1960.

John Coltrane

Carno, Zita. "The Style of John Coltrane." *Jazz Review* 2 (October 1959), 16–21; 2 (November 1959), 13–17.

Cole, William Shadrack. "The Style of John Coltrane, 1955–1967." Ph.D. dissertation, Wesleyan University, 1974.

Coltrane, John and Don DeMichael. "Coltrane on Coltrane." *down beat* 27 (September 29, 1960), 26–27.

Hentoff, Nat. Record liner notes to *Meditations* by John Coltrane. Impulse A–9110, 1966.

Kofsky, Frank. "John Coltrane." In *Black Giants.* Edited by Pauline Rivelli and Robert Levin. New York: World, 1970.

Mathieu, Bill. A review of *Ascension* by John Coltrane (Impulse AS–95, 1965). In *down beat* 33 (May 5, 1966), 25.

Simpkins, Cuthbert O. *Coltrane.* New York: Herndon House, 1975.

Thomas, J. C. *Chasin' the Trane: The Music and Mystique of John Coltrane.* Garden City, N.Y.: Doubleday, 1975.

Turner, Richard. "John Coltrane: A Biographical Sketch." *Black Perspective in Music* 3 (Spring 1975), 3–16.

Williams, Martin T. "John Coltrane: Man in the Middle." *down beat* 34 (December 14, 1967), 15–17.

Miles Davis

Albertson, Chris. "Unmasking of Miles Davis." *Saturday Review* 54 (November 27, 1971), 67–69.

Cole, Bill. *Miles Davis: A Musical Biography*. New York: Morrow, 1974.

DeMichael, Don. "Miles Davis," *Rolling Stone* 48 (December 13, 1969), 23–26.

Feather, Leonard. "Miles." In *From Satchmo to Miles*. New York: Stein & Day, 1972.

Gardner, Barbara. "The Enigma of Miles Davis." *down beat* 27 (January 7, 1960), 20–23.

Hall, Gregg. "Miles: Today's Most Influential Contemporary Musician." *down beat* 41 (July 18, 1974), 16.

Kerschbaumer, Franz. "Zum Personalstil von Miles Davis." *Jazzforschung* 3 (1971–72), 225–32.

Korall, Burt. " The Davis Phenomenon." *Saturday Review* 51 (February 10, 1968), 50–51.

McRae, Barry. "Avant Courier: Miles Davis — Since Philharmonia Hall, Berlin, 1964." *Jazz Journal* 28 (June 1975), 10–12.

Williams, Martin T. "Miles Davis: Conception in Search of a Sound." *Jazz* 4 (October 1965), 8–11.

Don Ellis

Balleras, Jon. A review of *The New Rhythm Book* by Don Ellis (North Hollywood, Calif.: Ellis Music Enterprises, 1972). In *down beat* 40 (November 22, 1973), 34.

Bessom, Malcolm E. "Don Ellis and 'The New Thing.'" *Jazz* 2 (September 1963), 10–11.

Diehl, Digby. Record liner notes to *Electric Bath* by Don Ellis. Columbia CS–9585, 1968.

Ellis, Don. *The New Rhythm Book*. North Hollywood, Calif.: Ellis Music Enterprises, 1972.

Feather, Leonard. "Don Ellis." In *From Satchmo to Miles*. New York: Stein & Day, 1972.

Willard, Patricia. "This Is the Don Ellis Interview." *down beat* 41 (January 31, 1974), 14–15.

Duke Ellington

Dance, Stanley. *The World of Duke Ellington.* New York: Scribner, 1970.

Ellington, Edward Kennedy (Duke). *Music Is My Mistress.* Garden City, N.Y.: Doubleday, 1973.

Yusef Lateef

Hammer, Robert. Record liner notes to *1984* by Yusef Lateef. Impulse S–84, 1966.

Morgenstern, Dan. A review of *A Flat, G Flat and C* by Yusef Lateef (Impulse AS–9117, 1966). In *down beat* 33 (November 3, 1966), 28.

Nelson, Don. A review of *1984* by Yusef Lateef (Impulse S–84, 1966). In *down beat* 33 (April 7, 1966), 27–28.

Welding, Pete. "Music as Color: Yusef Lateef." *down beat* 32 (May 20, 1965), 20–22.

Charles Mingus

Berendt, Joachim-Ernst. "Mingus and the Shadow of Duke Ellington." Translated by Nigel Whittaker. *Jazz* 4 (April 1965), 17–19.

Dance, Stanley. "Mingus Speaks." *Jazz* 2 (November 1963), 11.

Litweiler, John B. "There's a Mingus among Us." *down beat* 42 (February 27, 1975), 12.

Archie Shepp

Griffith, Pat. Record liner notes to *Live at the Pan-African Festival* by Archie Shepp. Actuel 51, 1969.

Hentoff, Nat. "Archie Shepp: The Way Ahead." In *Black Giants.* Edited by Pauline Rivelli and Robert Levin. New York: World, 1970.

Jones, LeRoi. "Voice from the Avant Garde: Archie Shepp." *down beat* 32 (January 14, 1965), 18.

Litweiler, John B. "Shepp: An Old Schoolmaster in a Brown Suit." *down beat* 41 (November 7, 1974), 15.

McRae, Barry. "Avant Courier: The Traditionalism of Archie Shepp." *Jazz Journal* 28 (September 1975), 14.

Shepp, Archie. "An Artist Speaks Bluntly." *down beat* 32 (December 16, 1965), 11.

———. "On Jazz." *Jazz* 4 (August 1965), 24.

———. "A View from the Inside." In *Down Beat Music '66* (1966 Yearbook).

Wilmer, Valerie. "The Fire This Time." In *Jazz People*. Indianapolis: Bobbs-Merrill, 1970.

Sun Ra

Figi, J. B. Record liner notes to *Sun Song* by Sun Ra. Delmark 411, 1965.

Fiofori, Tam. "Sun Ra's Space Odyssea." *down beat* 37 (May 14, 1970), 14–17.

McRae, Barry. "Sun Ra." *Jazz Journal* 30 (August 1966), 15–16.

Russo, William. A review of *Fate Is a Pleasant Mood* (Saturn 9956–2–B), *The Magic City* (Saturn 711), and *The Heliocentric Worlds of Sun Ra*, Vol. II (ESP–1017) by Sun Ra. In *down beat* 33 (October 6, 1966), 32.

Townley, Ray. "Sun Ra." *down beat* 40 (December 20, 1973), 18.

Cecil Taylor

Figi, J. B. "Cecil Taylor: African Code, Black Methodology." *down beat* 42 (April 10, 1975), 12.

Hentoff, Nat. "The Persistent Challenge of Cecil Taylor." *down beat* 32 (February 25, 1965), 17.

Spellman, A. B. "Cecil Taylor." In *Black Music: Four Lives*. 2d ed. New York: Schocken, 1970.

Taylor, Cecil. Record liner notes to *Unit Structures* by Cecil Taylor. Blue Note 84237, 1966.

Wilmer, Valerie. "Each Man His Own Academy." In *Jazz People*. Indianapolis: Bobbs-Merrill, 1970.

BIBLIOGRAPHY

Other Musicians

Barkan, Todd. "Rahsaan Speaks His Peace." *down beat* 41 (August 15, 1974), 13.

Coltrane, Alice. Record liner notes to *Journey in Satchidananda* by Alice Coltrane. Impulse AS–9203, 1970.

Dance, Stanley. "A Jazz Musician in Africa: Randy Weston." *Jazz* 4 (April 1965), 25–26.

DeMichael, Don. "A Long Look at Stan Getz." *down beat* 33 (June 2, 1966), 15–17.

Feather, Leonard. "Dave Brubeck, Composer." *down beat* 33 (June 30, 1966), 18–20.

Fowler, William L. "Oliver Nelson: New Hope for the Abstract Truth." *down beat* 42 (April 24, 1975), 10.

Hennessey, Mike. "The Emancipation of Elvin Jones." *down beat* 33 (March 1966), 23–24.

Hentoff, Nat. "Leon Thomas: Spirits Known and Unknown." In *Black Giants*. Edited by Pauline Rivelli and Robert Levin. New York: World, 1970.

Jones, Olive. "Conversation with George Russell: A New Theory for Jazz." *Black Perspective in Music* 2 (Spring 1974), 63–74.

Kettle, Rupert. "Re: Elvin Jones — A Technical Analysis of the Poll-Winning Drummer's Recorded Solo." *down beat* 33 (August 11, 1966), 17–19.

Levin, Robert. Record liner notes to *Eric Dolphy in Europe*, Vol. I, by Eric Dolphy. Prestige PR–7304, 1963.

———. "Sunny Murray: The Continuous Crackling of Glass." In *Black Giants*. Edited by Pauline Rivelli and Robert Levin. New York: World, 1970.

Mehegan, John. "Bill Evans: An Interview." *Jazz* 4 (January 1965), 5.

———. "Discussion: Herbie Hancock Talks to John Mehegan." *Jazz* 3 (September 1964), 23.

Mitchell, Charles. "The Anatomical Signatures of Airto." *down beat* 41 (November 7, 1974), 18.

Newman, Peter. "Stan Kenton: Speaks Out." *down beat* 40 (December 20, 1973), 19.

Rivelli, Pauline. "Alice Coltrane." In *Black Giants*. Edited by Pauline Rivelli and Robert Levin. New York: World, 1970.

———. "Oliver Nelson's African Tour: Interview." In *Black Giants*. Edited by Pauline Rivelli and Robert Levin. New York: World, 1970.

Schaffer, Jim. "The Perspective of Frank Zappa." *down beat* 40 (September 13, 1973), 14.

Simosko, Vladimir and Barry Tepperman. *Eric Dolphy: A Musical Biography and Discography*. Washington, D.C.: Smithsonian Institution Press, 1974.

Stephens, Lorin. "The Passionate Conviction: Jimmy Giuffre." *Jazz Review* 3 (February 1960), 6–11.

Stephenson, Gene. "Conversation with Andrew Cyrille: Dialogue of the Drums." *Black Perspective in Music* 3 (Spring 1975), 53–57.

Thorne, Francis. "An Afternoon with John Lewis." *Jazz Review* 3 (March 1960), 6–9.

Toner, John. "Chick Corea." *down beat* 41 (March 28, 1974), 14–16.

Underwood, Lee. "McCoy Tyner: Savant of the Astral Latitudes." *down beat* 42 (September 11, 1975), 12.

Willard, Patricia. "Paul Horn and the Time Barrier." *Jazz* 5 (October 1966), 11–13.

Wilmer, Valerie. "Back to the African Heart Beat (Randy Weston)." In *Jazz People*. Indianapolis: Bobbs-Merrill, 1970.

Addenda

Arnold, Augustus. Record liner notes to *The Lowlands* by Archie Shepp and Philly Joe Jones. Fantasy 86018, 1969.

Baraka, Imamu Amiri (LeRoi Jones). *The Autobiography of LeRoi Jones*. New York: Freundlich Books, 1984.

———. "The Phenomenon of *Soul* in African-American Music." *The Music: Reflections on Jazz and Blues*. New York: William Morrow, 1987.

Beauchamp, L. T. (Chicago Beau). Record liner notes to *The Lowlands* by Archie Shepp and Philly Joe Jones. Fantasy 86018, 1969.

Benston, Kimberly W., ed. *Imamu Amiri Baraka (LeRoi Jones): A Collection of Critical Essays*. Englewood Cliffs, N.J.: Prentice-Hall, 1978.

Brown, Lloyd W. *Amiri Baraka*. Boston: Twayne, 1980.

Brubeck, Dave. Record liner notes to *Jazz Impressions of Japan* by the Dave Brubeck Quartet. Columbia PC 9012, 1964.

Collier, James Lincoln. *The Making of Jazz: A Comprehensive History*. Boston: Houghton Mifflin, 1978.

Coltrane, Alice. Record liner notes to *Journey in Satchidananda* by Alice Coltrane. Impulse AS 9203, 1970.

Coltrane, John. "A Love Supreme," in record liner notes to *A Love Supreme* by John Coltrane. Impulse S–77, 1964.

Dance, Stanley. Record liner notes to *New Orleans Suite* by Duke Ellington. Atlantic SD–1580, 1971.

———. Record liner notes to *Third Sacred Concert: The Majesty of God* by Duke Ellington. RCA SF 8406, 1973.

De Lerma, Dominique-René. Record liner notes to *Afro-American Symphony* by William Grant Still et al. Columbia M 32782, 1974.

Ellington, Edward Kennedy. Record liner notes to *Second Sacred Concert* by Duke Ellington. Prestige P–24045, n.d.

Evans, David. "Black American Music as a Symbol of Identity." *Jazzforschung* 13 (1981), 105–16.

Feather, Leonard. Record liner notes to *Odyssey of Iska* by Wayne Shorter. Blue Note 84363, 1970.

Finn, Julio. Record liner notes to *The Lowlands* by Archie Shepp and Philly Joe Jones. Fantasy 86018, 1969.

Hancock, Herbie. Record liner notes to *Maiden Voyage* by Herbie Hancock. Blue Note BLP–84195, 1965.

Harrison, Max. "Jazz." *The New Grove Gospel, Blues and Jazz*. New York: Macmillan, 1986.

Hentoff, Nat. Record liner notes to *Fire Music* by Archie Shepp. Impulse AS–86, 1965.

Jordan, Jennifer. "Cultural Nationalism in the 1960s: Politics and Poetry." In *Race, Politics, and Culture: Critical Essays on the Radicalism of the 1960s.* Edited by Adolph Reed, Jr. Westport, Ct.: Greenwood Press, 1986.

Keepnews, Orrin. Record liner notes to *Freedom Suite* by Sonny Rollins. Riverside OJC–067/RLP–258, 1958.

Kelly, Nora. Record liner notes to *Maiden Voyage* by Herbie Hancock. Blue Note BLP–84195, 1965.

Litweiler, John. *The Freedom Principle: Jazz after 1958.* New York: William Morrow, 1984.

Lyons, Len. *The 101 Best Jazz Albums: A History of Jazz on Records.* New York: William Morrow, 1980.

Meyer, Leonard B. *Music, the Arts, and Ideas: Patterns and Predictions in Twentieth-Century Culture.* Chicago: University of Chicago Press, 1967.

Nelson, Oliver. Record liner notes to *Afro/American Sketches* by Oliver Nelson. Prestige 7225, 1961.

Newton, Francis. *The Jazz Scene.* London: MacGibbon & Kee, 1959.

Palmer, Robert. Record liner notes to *Paul Horn in India* by Paul Horn and native Indian instrumentalists. Blue Note LA529–H2, reissued 1975.

Rivelli, Pauline. "Alice Coltrane Interview." In *Black Giants.* Edited by Pauline Rivelli and Robert Levin. New York: World, 1970.

Rollins, Sonny. Record liner notes to *Freedom Suite* by Sonny Rollins. Riverside OJC–067/RLP–258, 1958.

Shepp, Archie. Record liner notes to *Live at the Donaueschingen Festival* by Archie Shepp. Impulse AS–XX.

Shorter, Wayne. Record liner notes to *Odyssey of Iska* by Wayne Shorter. Blue Note 84363, 1970.

Tesser, Neil. Record liner notes to *The Far East Suite* by Duke Ellington. LPM/LSP–3782, 1966; reissued Bluebird 7640–1–RB, 1988.

Tyner, McCoy. Record liner notes to *Extensions* by McCoy Tyner. Blue Note LA006G, 1970.

Young, Steve. Record liner notes to *The New Wave in Jazz* by various artists. Impulse A–90, 1965.

Index